Rapidly Prototyping Interfaces with InDesign

Rapidly Prototyping Interfaces with InDesign

Carla Viviana Coleman

CRC Press
Taylor & Francis Group
Boca Raton London New York

CRC Press is an imprint of the
Taylor & Francis Group, an **informa** business

A CHAPMAN & HALL BOOK

CRC Press
Taylor & Francis Group
6000 Broken Sound Parkway NW, Suite 300
Boca Raton, FL 33487-2742

© 2018 by Taylor & Francis Group, LLC
CRC Press is an imprint of Taylor & Francis Group, an Informa business

No claim to original U.S. Government works

Printed on acid-free paper

International Standard Book Number-13: 978-1-1384-8638-6 (Hardback)
International Standard Book Number-13: 978-1-4987-9924-9 (Paperback)

Visit the Taylor & Francis Web site at
http://www.taylorandfrancis.com

and the CRC Press Web site at
http://www.crcpress.com

Contents

Section I   Setting Up

Section II   Importing Files

Section III   Recipes for Interactive Prototypes

Section IV   Exporting Testing-Ready Prototypes (and Other Export Options)

SECTION I
Setting Up

1

InDesign Workspace

This introduction to InDesign provides basic information on aspects such as tools, menus, windows, workspace, and layout. InDesign has evolved tremendously since its launch in 2000. Version 1.0 had considerable limitations but provided what was needed at that time in the print design world. However, over time, InDesign has become multifaceted and is now able to create not only design files for print but also files that have animation and interactivity, for various types of devices.

Installing InDesign

To purchase InDesign, you have to visit adobe.com. Once the application is downloaded through the Creative Cloud, you can see it in your Applications folder and start working with it (Figures 1.1 through 1.3).

Figure 1.1

Installing the Creative Cloud icon on your desktop after downloading the Adobe Cloud package.

Figure 1.2

Folder application location.

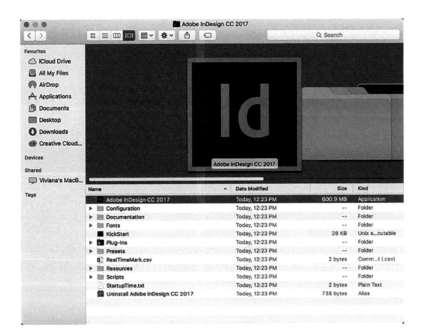

Figure 1.3

The folder in which InDesign is located after downloading the app.

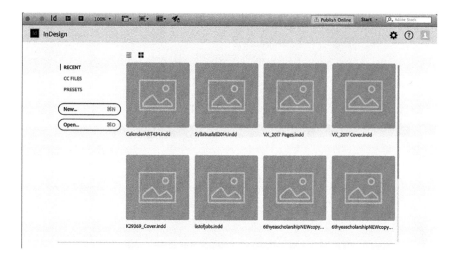

Figure 1.4

Start window when the InDesign application is open.

When you open InDesign, you will be able to see your previous files. However, if this is the first time that you have used InDesign, you will not see anything on the right-hand side. The left-hand menu reads Recent, CC Files, Presets, New, and Open (Figure 1.4).

You can open files in five ways:

1. *Recent*: You can see your files on the right-hand side.
2. *CC Files* are files that you have saved in the Adobe Creative Cloud. Saving CC files on the Creative Cloud when collaborating in a team is helpful because you can work on the same document at the same time. When the document is saved, you instantly see the changes, even if you are remotely connected.
3. With *Presets*: You are able to choose the paper size or screen size you desire.
4. *New* allows you to customize the size of the file for print, web, or mobile (Figure 1.5).

In addition, you can set the number of pages and the width, height, columns, margins, bleeds (space outside the margins), and slugs (area outside the page including the bleed). If you choose web or mobile, InDesign automatically sets the measurement in pixels (px) for screens and digital environments. Once all the settings have been chosen, you can click OK and move onto the next step, which is the creation of the canvas file that you will be working on.

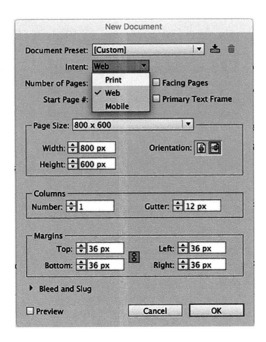

Figure 1.5

Creating a new document in InDesign.

Preview checkbox.

Toward the bottom of the left-hand side, you can see the preview checkbox, which allows you to see the settings of the document.

5. *Open* allows you to open a previous InDesign file that you have worked with. If you open any file that is InDesign CS5, CS6, CS7, CS8, or CS9 and CC 2014, CC 2015, CC 2016, or CC 2017, make sure the file was saved with the extension *.idml,* which allows this file to open in various versions of InDesign.

The best option to choose to organize the menu you want to work with is by going into *Window>Workspace>* and selecting the environment: *Advanced, Book, Digital Publishing, Essentials, Interactive for PDF, Printing and Proofing, and Typography* (Figure 1.6).

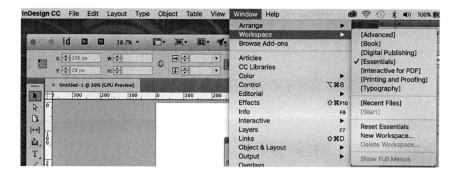

Figure 1.6

Setting and choosing the right workspace in InDesign.

Figure 1.7

Top bar in the Window menu.

These options only allow you access to certain tools faster. If you are starting to create interactivity in InDesign, start with *Interactive for PDF* on the menu because this provides you with the necessary tools to start. You can switch to any of the options mentioned earlier anytime (Figure 1.7).

This allows you to go directly to several places in a short period of time. From left to right: Bridge (an Adobe application that allows you to manage your files), Stock (an Adobe application that allows you to search for images), Zooming in and out, View options, Screen mode, Arrange documents, GPU performance is enabled, Publish online, Workspace tool reset option, and Search bar that goes directly to Adobe Stock Photos (you need to become a member to download photos).

How to Bring Tool Windows to the Workspace?

Every tool option is available in the Window option located on the top toolbar. In the above-mentioned image, the Color option is selected; this goes into a sub-menu that provides four more options: Adobe Color Themes, Color, Gradient, and Swatches (Figure 1.8).

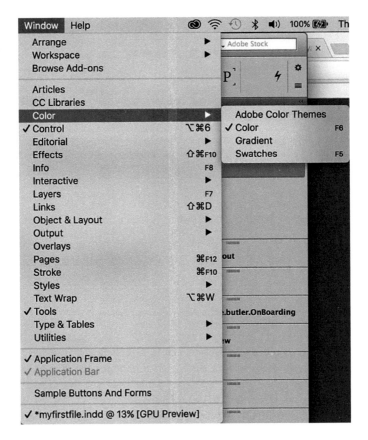

Figure 1.8

Tools in InDesign under the Window option.

Main Tools and Menu Options

InDesign provides a toolbar on the left-hand side that helps us to add text, shapes, lines, gradients, cuts, and transforms. Meanwhile, the menus on the right-hand side have more menus with options that can be used according to your planned design (Figure 1.9).

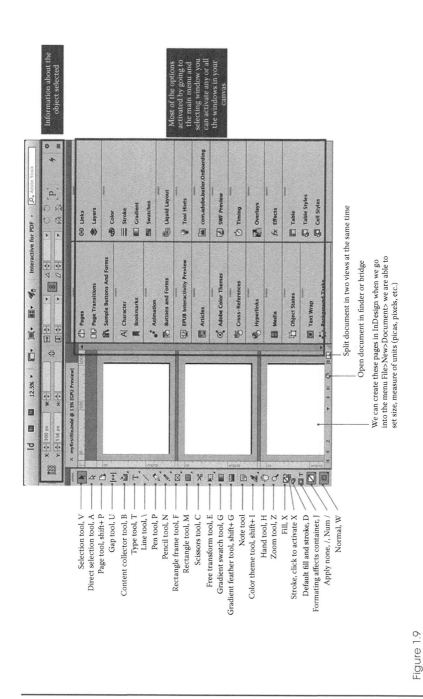

Information about the object selected

Most of the options activated by going to the main menu and selecting window you can activate any or all the windows in your canvas

Selection tool, V
Direct selection tool, A
Page tool, shift+ P
Gap tool, U
Content collector tool, B
Type tool, T
Line tool, \
Pen tool, P
Pencil tool, N
Rectangle frame tool, F
Rectangle tool, M
Scissors tool, C
Free transform tool, E
Gradient swatch tool, G
Gradient feather tool, shift+ G
Note tool
Color theme tool, shift+ I
Hand tool, H
Zoom tool, Z
Fill, X
Stroke, click to activate X
Default fill and stroke, D
Formating affects container, J
Apply none, /, Num /
Normal, W

Split document in two views at the same time

Open document in finder or bridge

We can create these pages in InDesign when we go into the menu File>New>Document> we are able to set size, measure of units (picas, pixels, etc.)

Figure 1.9
Several tools in InDesign are shown from the selection tool to animation.

2

Interactivity

When creating an interactive document, it is necessary to first decide whether it will be *web*, *mobile*, or a *custom size*. It is very hard to make this change afterward, because you will have to redo everything, including the layout. When prototyping for digital interfaces, if the document size changes, the grid structure and layout also must change, which is more challenging than it seems. It is important to consider user functionality. For example, a phone app prototype will have a drastically different layout on an iPad, let alone on a desktop. Therefore, it is important to sketch your paper prototype before jumping into the final document size (Figures 2.1 through 2.3).

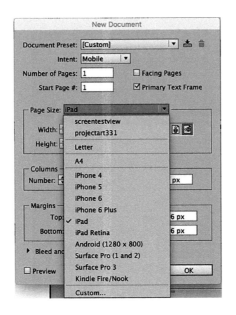

Figure 2.1

New Document Window > Intent > Select > Mobile. Then, select the Page Size options including the Custom option at the bottom.

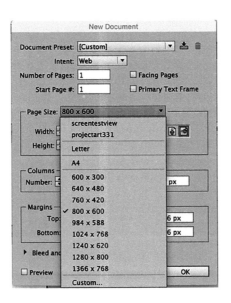

Figure 2.2

New Document Window > Intent > Select > Web. Then, select the Page Size options including the Custom option at the bottom.

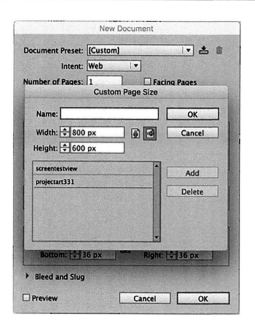

Figure 2.3

Custom Page Size settings.

From New Document > Page Size > Select, the "Custom Page Size" drop-down menu allows you to decide the width and height and whether you want the document in a vertical or horizontal position according to these width and height values. In addition, you can add or delete any sizes previously customized.

Preset and Custom Sizes

The only difference between web, mobile, and custom size is the preset sizes given and your own customized sizes. A wide range of options for setting up the correct size of document are available at http://screensiz.es/ (see "Screen Sizes | Viewport Sizes and Pixel Densities for Popular Devices") (Figure 2.4).

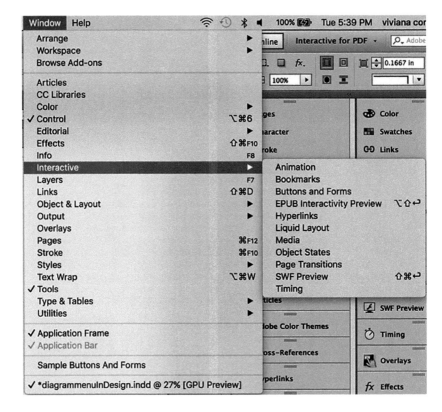

Figure 2.4

Choosing from the interactive options located under "Window."

Tools

The tools you will be using are broad according to the purpose of the design. If you want interactive menus or content, go to "Window" and select "Interactive." This option provides several options: Animation, Bookmarks, Button and Forms, EPUB Interactivity Preview, Hyperlinks, Liquid Layout, Media, Object States, Page Transitions, small web format (SWF), and Timing.

Export

Types of files to export:

1. PDF Interactive
2. EPS
3. EPUB (Fixed Layout)
4. EPUB (Reflowable)
5. Flash CS6 Professional (FLA)
6. Flash Player (SWF)
7. HTML
8. Publish online

SECTION II
Importing Files

3

Photoshop

Saving Files in Photoshop

Tips for Reducing Your File Size

When working with images for interfaces, smaller is better, because computers' loading time and memory vary, and a light and agile prototype is preferable.

Please read the following tips:

1. Merge and flatten images. Do not keep layers. Save a copy to keep the original layers as a backup.
2. Layer masks take a lot of memory space. Try not to include them in your files.
3. Rasterizing Smart objects makes a file smaller.

Converting a Photoshop Image into a JPEG

Please follow Figures 3.1 through 3.4. Then, select JPEG from the options at the top right of the pop-up window, "Save for Web."

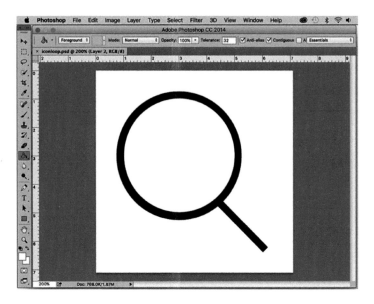

Figure 3.1

Once an image has been created in Photoshop, the next step is to save the image.

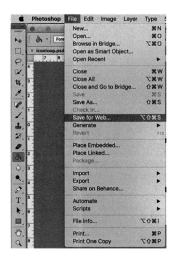

Figure 3.2

In Photoshop, go to "File" from the top menu and select "Save for Web."

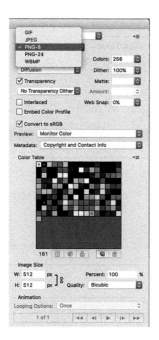

Figure 3.3

At the top left of the window, the preset options allow saving the image in the following formats: GIF, JPEG, PNG-8, PNG-24, and Wireless Application Protocol Bitmap (WBMP). Please check with the Human-Centered Design Guidelines.

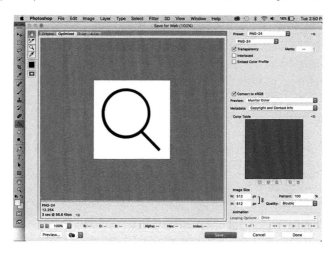

Figure 3.4

A window titled "Save for Web" shows the image on the left. Here, you can change the size, resolution, and quality of the image. Once you have selected the settings desired, click "Save" in the bottom-right corner.

Converting a Photoshop Image into a PNG

Please follow Figures 3.2 through 3.4. Then, select PNG from the options at the top right of the pop-up window, "Save for Web."

Converting a Photoshop Image to a *Scalable Vector Graphics*

The plugin for Photoshop titled "Photoshop SVG export 4.0" allows you to export Scalable Vector Graphics (SVG) images out of Photoshop. Check your version of Photoshop and whether this plugin can be installed to match the version you have.

Icon Preparation for Mac OS X, Using iTunes Icon as an Example

Figure 3.5.

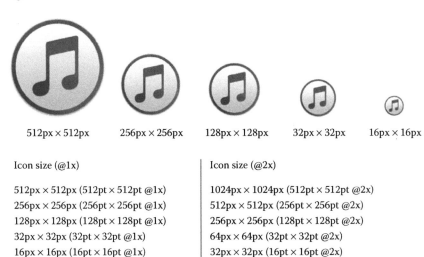

| 512px × 512px | 256px × 256px | 128px × 128px | 32px × 32px | 16px × 16px |

Icon size (@1x)	Icon size (@2x)
512px × 512px (512pt × 512pt @1x)	1024px × 1024px (512pt × 512pt @2x)
256px × 256px (256pt × 256pt @1x)	512px × 512px (256pt × 256pt @2x)
128px × 128px (128pt × 128pt @1x)	256px × 256px (128pt × 128pt @2x)
32px × 32px (32pt × 32pt @1x)	64px × 64px (32pt × 32pt @2x)
16px × 16px (16pt × 16pt @1x)	32px × 32px (16pt × 16pt @2x)

Figure 3.5

iTunes icon, part of the Mac OS X system that uses five sizes in two versions: 1x (standard devices) and 2x (a larger version than the standard). These icons need to be set to these sizes to allow the app to run smoothly in Mac OS X. (Courtesy of iTunes.)

Bringing Images from Photoshop into InDesign

The cursor must be where you want to place the image on the selected page. The pop-up window titled "Place" (Figure 3.6)—Mac users, press Command+D and PC users, press Windows+D—will give you access to your computer's files to find the correct image. If you are trying to Place images from the web, such as from an email or a website, you must first save the image to your computer. Images from outside your computer system cannot be accessed (Figures 3.7 and 3.8).

Figure 3.6

Pop-up window in InDesign titled "Place."

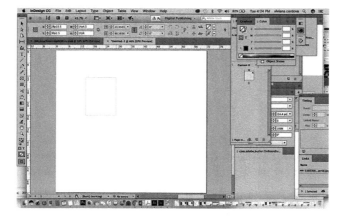

Figure 3.7

Once the image has been selected, the cursor will show you a preview of the image, creating a rectangle where the image will be placed.

Figure 3.8

Once the shape has been created, the image will automatically be placed on the page in InDesign. (Courtesy of UMBC.)

Icons and JPEG Images

Once Photoshop files are imported into InDesign, you should create categories based on the purpose of the image: icon, photo for a gallery, background image, or VR 360° image. Each type of image will vary in size, as follows:

1. An icon needs to be small; take note of the exact pixel sizes of all images.
2. Photos for a gallery should have good resolution, but this will vary if they are part of a web app. If the app is for the web, the photos definitely must be smaller and most likely a.png compared with an app nested in a device that provides high-quality images. Having said that, the developer may require images in PNG format. Agree on this with the developer, because these two mediums are completely different. Therefore, ask the developer for confirmation on how the files should be prepared. In particular, VR 360° images are very large because they are panoramic.

The images in e-books must be JPEG and high resolution. They need not be 300 DPI, but they do have to maintain their quality, which will vary from project to project. If you are creating a photo e-book, work with the standard limitations (around 650 MB on some e-readers, such as Kindles) because of the high resolutions of modern e-reader screens. You do not want the images to crash the e-book, so manage the images properly and find a good balance that fits the e-book you are creating.

Watch for Pixelation

When a small image is then enlarged, it will look pixelated. Therefore, aim to work with high-resolution images. Do not force an image to be a size it is not meant to be, as this will weaken the design and the content. The image will not be proportionally placed and might lack resolution.

Managing Your Files in InDesign

We often lose track of how many images are in an InDesign document; therefore, it is helpful to track the images by selecting Window and then Links from the top menu (Figures 3.9 through 3.11).

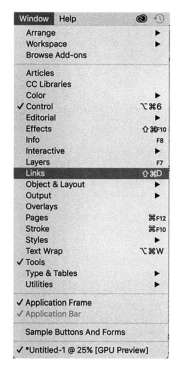

Figure 3.9

From the top menu, select "Window" and then "Links."

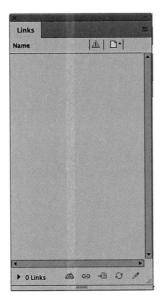

Figure 3.10

When there are no images or any types of files, including movies or sounds, the "Links" window will be empty.

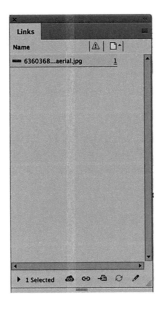

Figure 3.11

If InDesign recognizes an image or another type of file, it will be shown under "Links." Here, we see a JPEG image in the InDesign document.

Operating Systems

Every operating system has different resolutions and limitations for all types of images, including icon sizes. In Photoshop, images can be saved at various resolutions and sizes so that you can test them and decide which has the best quality for your design, especially if you are working with photographs. In addition, due to the various types of sizes and resolutions, the icons will require export at various sizes to adapt to different types of screens (see Figure 3.5). The example in Figure 3.12 shows the guidelines for Android.

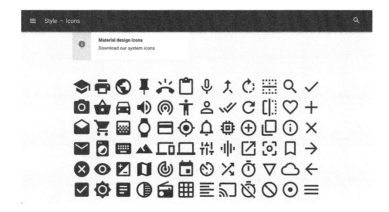

Figure 3.12

Material design icons already provided by Android. (Courtesy of Material Design. Icons—Style—System Icons. Accessed January 5, 2017, https://material.io/guidelines/style/icons.html#icons-system-icons.)

Icons for Android

Figures 3.13 and 3.14.

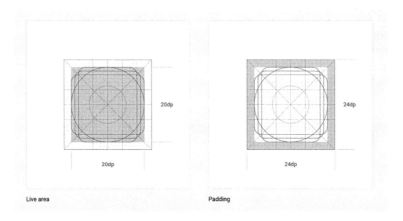

Figure 3.13

Icon guidelines, including padding. The least space allowed around the icon. (Courtesy of Material Design. Icons—Style—System Icons. Accessed January 5, 2017, https://material.io/guidelines/style/icons.html#icons-system-icons.)

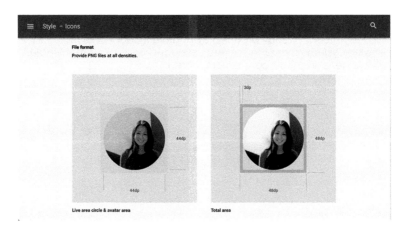

Figure 3.14

Avatar PNG image limitations according to the Android operating system. (Courtesy of Material Design. Icons—Style—System Icons. Accessed January 5, 2017, https://material.io/guidelines/style/icons.html#icons-system-icons.)

Panorama options (http://wiki.panotools.org/Panorama_formats) (Figures 3.15 and 3.16).

Figure 3.15

Image using VR and 360° in a panoramic format. (Courtesy of WordPress. Introducing VR and 360° Content for All WordPress.com Sites. Accessed December 15, 2016, https://en.blog.wordpress.com/2016/12/15/introducing-vr-and-360-content-for-all-wordpress-com-sites.)

Figure 3.16

Using a vector image that is landscape size. (Courtesy of Pixabay. Accessed January 5, 2017, https://pixabay.com/en/users/jschofield-1411206.)

Bibliography

Material Design. Icons—Style—System Icons. Accessed January 5, 2017, https://material.io/guidelines/style/icons.html#icons-system-icons.

Pixabay. Accessed January 5, 2017, https://pixabay.com/en/users/jschofield-1411206.

WordPress. Introducing VR and 360° Content for All WordPress.com Sites. Accessed December 15, 2016, https://en.blog.wordpress.com/2016/12/15/introducing-vr-and-360-content-for-all-wordpress-com-sites.

4

Illustrator

With Illustrator, you can work with vector images. These types of images are always smaller, because they use vector points instead of pixels, as in Photoshop.

What Are Vector Files?

Vector files are created based on polygons and mathematical curves and lines. No matter the size, whether reduced or enlarged, they maintain the sharpest quality. By contrast, Photoshop uses pixels, meaning that once an image is small, it cannot be enlarged to high quality, because the limited pixels means the image will always have low resolution.

Vectors are preferred for icons, shapes, and even typefaces that need sharpness around the outline. In Illustrator, vector files with the extensions. AI, .EPS, and .PDF can be exported as pixelated images, such as JPEG, PNG, and GIF. This flexibility gives you a broader ability to work with files to add in InDesign.

Saving Files in Illustrator

When your file is ready, note its details by going to "File" on the top menu, then "Document Setup" and "Edit Artboards." A dashed line will run around your document. Then, press "Enter." A window titled "Artboard Options" will pop up. Here, you can make edits or take notes of the numerical values (width, height, vertical/horizontal orientation, etc.). Figures 4.1 through 4.6 show a final shape ready for use in an interface.

Figure 4.1

The vector image in this case is a simple shape that represents the "play" icon.

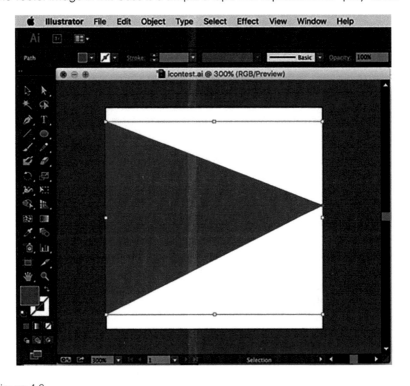

Figure 4.2

In this example, the vector file has three vector points (gray points) that form the shape.

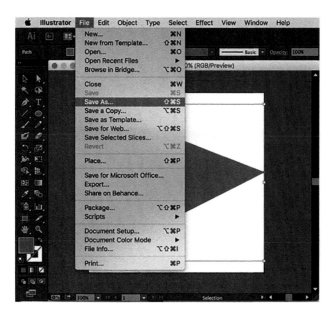

Figure 4.3

To save the file as a copy, select "File" from the top menu and "Save As."

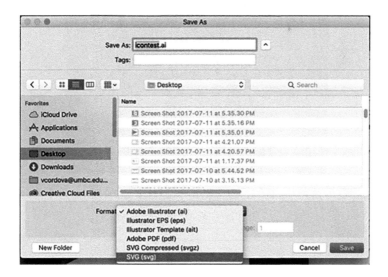

Figure 4.4

From the "Save As" window, you can change the name of the file. At the bottom is a drop-down menu from which you can choose from Adobe Illustrator (ai), Illustrator EPS (eps), Illustrator Template (ait), Adobe PDF (pdf), SVG Compressed (svgz), or SVG (svg) file formats.

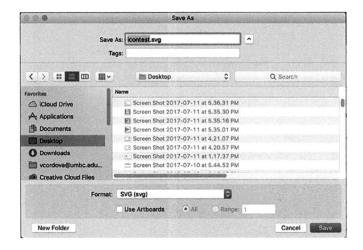

Figure 4.5

In this case, select SVG and click "Save."

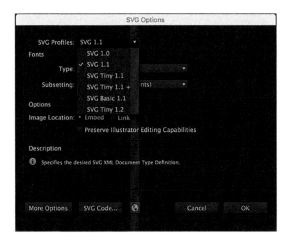

Figure 4.6

From the window titled "SVG Options," select SVG 1.1, which is the default option, and click "OK."

More about *Scalable Vector Graphics* Files

Scalable Vector Graphics (SVG) is a great option to keep icons at a high resolution while still maintaining a very small file size. Not all operating systems allow the use of SVG files, so check with your developer if this is a viable choice for your project. At present, SVG files are not supported in InDesign. SVG files are already being used on many platforms, such as e-books and websites, and their use will grow further in the future because of their flexibility.

Saving as a GIF, JPEG, and PNG

Figures 4.7 through 4.10.

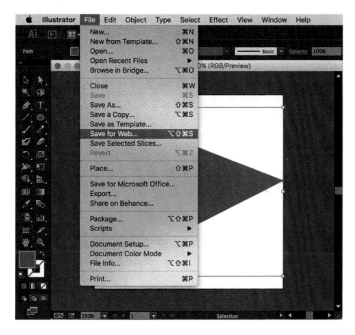

Figure 4.7

Select "File" from the top menu and then "Save for Web." This option is similar to the Photoshop "Save for Web."

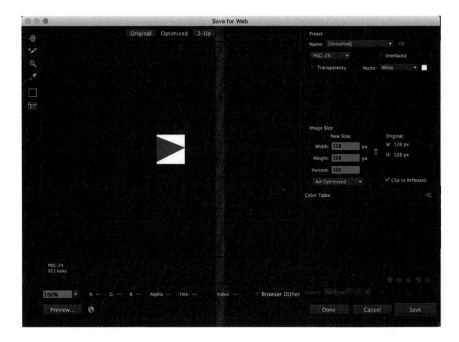

Figure 4.8

A window titled "Save for Web" will pop up. On the right side, there are several options. The type of file to export can be changed under "Preset," and the size can also be changed.

Figure 4.9

Preset provides four options: GIF, JPEG, PNG-8, and PNG-24. In this case, I selected the PNG-24 option, which provides transparency in the pixelated image.

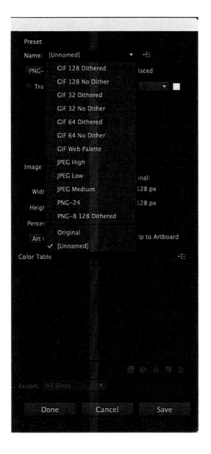

Figure 4.10

The above-mentioned option provides more detailed options of resolutions that will fit your needs: low to high resolution, JPEG to dithered (reduction in the number of colors), and not dithered (no reduction in the colors in an image).

Tips for Creating Icons in Illustrator

1. Use as few vector points as possible, because this creates a smoother shape.
2. Keep in mind the sizes of the icons you need. Ask yourself whether you need to create 10 different sizes or only 2. What matters is consistency and simplicity. When you require a wide range of sizes, the smaller the shape, the simpler it becomes. Simplifying the graphic makes it look

less crowded and busy when it becomes smaller, including any outline strokes. Visual consistency brings all icons together.

3. Make sure the metaphor (visual representation) makes sense for the image. Also, test your image with future users before making the final version (Figure 4.11).

Figure 4.11

Lock icon vector graphic. (typographyimages|Pixabay.)

Bringing Images from Illustrator into InDesign

Chapter 3 showed a similar process to the following steps. The main differences are the interface and capabilities of Illustrator, because it is software for making vector graphics.

Copy and Paste Option

Select the shape or group of shapes that you want to bring from Illustrator to InDesign by simply selecting the objects and copying and pasting. This option allows you to make edits inside the vector file in InDesign. The shapes brought into InDesign are not images; instead, they become vectors that are in the InDesign document (Figures 4.12 and 4.13).

Figure 4.12

Select the shape from Illustrator and press Command+C.

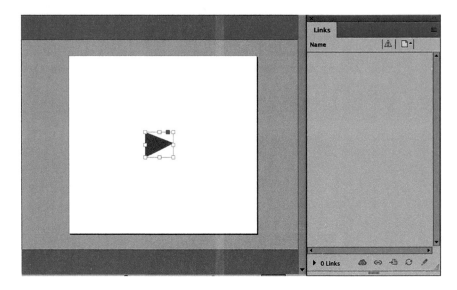

Figure 4.13

Go to InDesign and press Command+D in the document. Go to "Window" and open "Links" to see if the file is there. If it is not there, you can make any changes to maintain the vector quality of the shape.

Bringing an Image into InDesign with Place

See Figures 4.6 through 4.8 and 4.14.

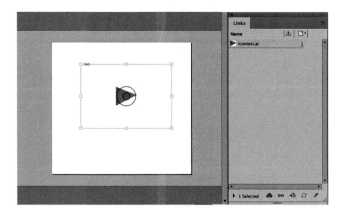

Figure 4.14

Place the image by using Command+D (Mac) or CTRL+D (PC). Although this file maintains the vector quality of the image, you cannot edit specific vector points of this shape when it is brought into InDesign as an image.

5

Audio

Audio can be useful in a design prototype for someone with visual disabilities or children learning pronunciation, for example. Sound can be an essential part of your project. In software such as Audition and Audacity, you can take sound you have recorded or purchased elsewhere and make edits before bringing it into InDesign. One of the most acceptable sound formats for InDesign is MP3. Keep in mind that some sound file formats might be too large or incompatible with flash and PDF files.

Sounds added to buttons or small transitions should be no longer than 0.5 of a second, settled, and suit the environment. If the sound is used for an audience of children, your design can be more flexible, because children prefer playful sounds with which they can interact. Test the sound with future users and seek feedback so you can make changes before your final version.

Sound Design Audio Library

If you have never used audio in prototypes before, you can access free or paid libraries that can save you time. If you are trying to record your own sound, start with the following options:

1. Free Sound at https://freesound.org/
2. Zapsplat at https://www.zapsplat.com/
3. Sound Bible at http://soundbible.com/free-sound-effects-1.html
4. Sonniss at http://www.sonniss.com/sound-effects/
5. Audio Micro at https://www.audiomicro.com/free-sound-effects
6. Sound Dogs at https://www.sounddogs.com/
7. Sound Effects Plus at https://www.soundeffectsplus.com/

Bringing Audio Files into InDesign

It is crucial to make sure the timing of sound fits with the content. For example, if you want an introduction, it is probably going to be long and will need to loop. But if you are using sound for a button or short transition, calculate the time and make it as effective as possible. Users will not wait too long, and you risk losing users with sounds that are too loud or too long. Overall, test your sound design with users before you make your final decision.

Adobe Audition CC

This software is part of the Adobe Creative Cloud. If you have an Adobe membership, you can download it easily from the Creative Cloud (Figures 5.1 through 5.6).

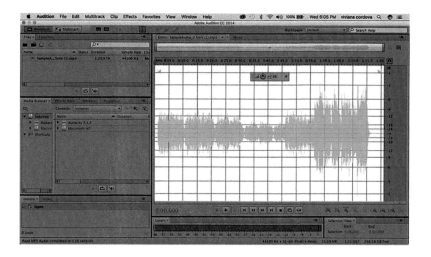

Figure 5.1

The Adobe Audition software interface provides a large canvas on the right where the sound wave can be edited.

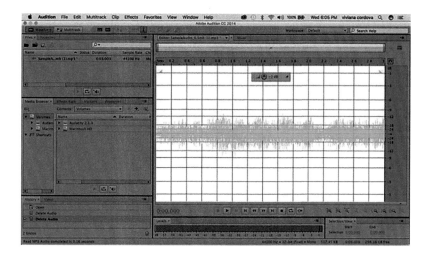

Figure 5.2

The screenshot of Audition shows the sound in Figure 5.1 edited to become a shorter version. The soundwave looks different when compared with the previous figure, because this sound is only a very small part of that in Figure 5.1.

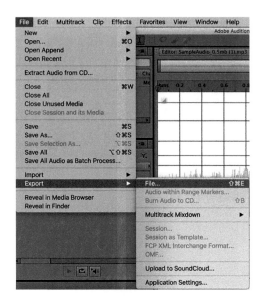

Figure 5.3

Once the sound you want to use is ready, select "File" from the top menu and then "Export" and "File."

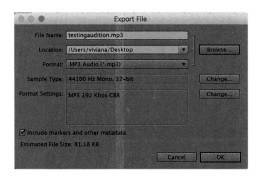

Figure 5.4

In the window titled "Export File," name the file and save it to the correct location on your computer. If you want to change the format settings, select "Change" from "Format Settings." Make sure you save the audio file in MP3 format.

Figure 5.5

Check that the File Format is MP3 and click "Save."

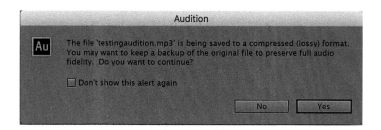

Figure 5.6

Another window will pop up reminding you that you have edited the file and asking you if you want to back up the previous file. If you do, click "Yes."

Bringing Files from Adobe Audition CC into InDesign

Audacity

This free sound software, which can be downloaded from http://www.audacity team.org/, allows you to edit and record any type of audio. It is compatible with Mac, PC, and Linux.

Raw File

When using Audacity, make sure you have the LAME plugin, which allows you to export MP3 files from Audacity. Download this plugin from http://lame. sourceforge.net/ (Figures 5.7 through 5.11).

Now, the MP3 audio file is available to bring into InDesign.

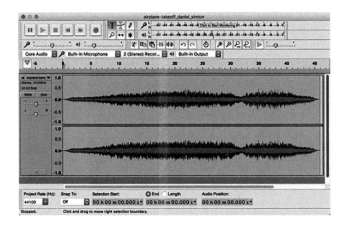

Figure 5.7

Audacity interface on a Mac with a raw file, 45 s long. We only need less than 3 s; therefore, it is necessary to cut the audio and select the right sound from this file.

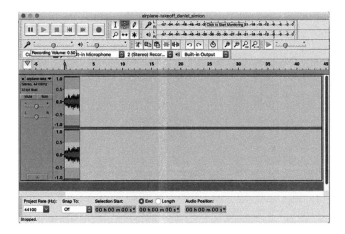

Figure 5.8

In this image, the audio lasts less than 3 s and has been edited to fit the needs of the InDesign project.

Figure 5.9

From the top menu, select "File" and "Export Audio."

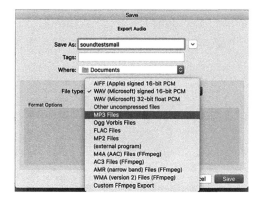

Figure 5.10

From the pop-up window titled "Save," give the audio file a name and location. Then, from the "File Type" drop-down menu, select "MP3 Files" and click "Save."

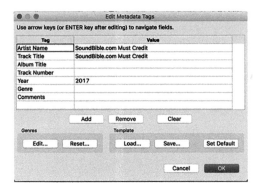

Figure 5.11

Another window pops up, titled "Edit Metadata Tags." In this example, we are using a sound from SoundBible.com and retaining the credit. If you created your own sound, then you can copyright it here. After you have entered all the information, click "OK."

Bringing Audio into InDesign

This method works similarly to bringing in images, with the only difference that the box of audio in InDesign is invisible. Only the diagonal blue lines inside the rectangle recognize the box as sound (Figures 5.12 through 5.14).

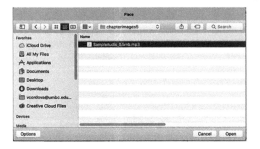

Figure 5.12

A window pops up titled "Place." Select the MP3 file you want to bring into the document in InDesign, SampleAudio_0.5mb.mp3 in this example.

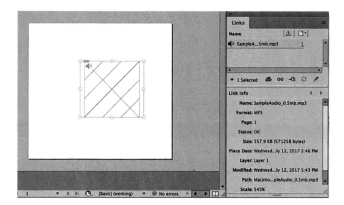

Figure 5.13

Create a square or rectangle, and the sound will automatically appear inside the shape. This method is similar to placing images from Photoshop and Illustrator (see Chapters 3 and 4). The audio file is listed inside the "Links" window on the right side.

Figure 5.14

Another way is to select "File" from the top menu and then click "Place," following the steps in Figures 5.6 and 5.7.

Checking the Sound in InDesign

Once sound has been brought into InDesign, it can be checked using the following steps (Figures 5.15 and 5.16).

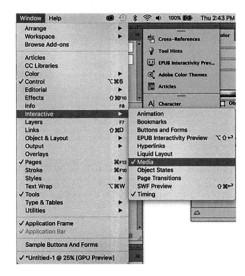

Figure 5.15

In InDesign, go to "Window" and select "Interactive" and then "Media."

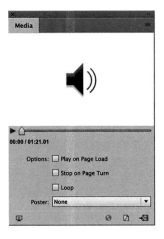

Figure 5.16

In the "Media" window, you can play the sound you brought into InDesign. You have three options: Play on Page Load, Stop on Page Turn, and Loop. You can preview these options by clicking on the bottom left icon (a TV screen with a play symbol in the middle).

Using Sound with Buttons

Using sound with buttons can be either annoying or helpful, depending on the audience. Children love sounds with buttons. However, someone in their 30s might not enjoy what a five-year-old enjoys. When adding sound to a button, the designer must thus choose carefully (Figures 5.17 through 5.26).

Figure 5.17

The sound can easily be added to the document by the same means as images. Outside the document canvas, in the gray area on the right side, the audio file is represented by the sound icon at the top-left corner of the image.

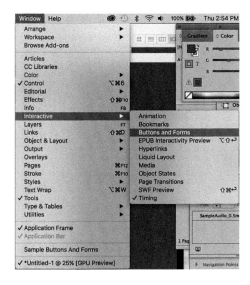

Figure 5.18

Go to the top menu and select "Window" and then "Interactive." From there, select "Buttons and Forms."

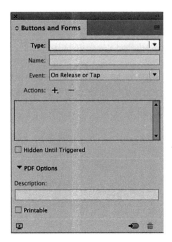

Figure 5.19

This window can be activated by selecting text or images. Anything on the canvas can be a button.

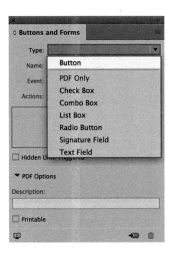

Figure 5.20

In the "Type" section, select the option needed from the drop-down menu. In the example case, "Button" is highlighted.

Figure 5.21

Under the "Name" section, name the button and select "On Release or Tap" under "Event." Other options might fit better your needs, such as "On Click," "On Rollover," "On Roll Off," "On Focus (PDF)," or "On Blur (PDF)." The options with "(PDF)" next to them only work for PDF files. All the other options work for small web format (SWF) files.

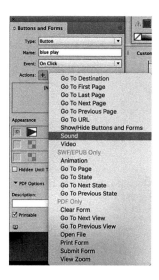

Figure 5.22

In the "Actions" section, the options are divided into different sections, highlighted in light gray as "SWF/EPUB Only" and "PDF Only." In this example, we are adding sound to a file that works in SWF/EPUB and PDF.

Figure 5.23

As the audio file has already been placed in the document, outside the canvas, InDesign detects the file and automatically offers the sounds as an option in the "Sound" section. Under "Options," select "Play."

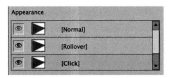

Figure 5.24

In the section "Appearance," activate one of the options: "Normal," "Rollover," or "Click."

Figure 5.25

The "Options" section provides various ways to assign an action to a button, such as Play, Stop, Pause, Resume, and Stop All (SWF only).

Figure 5.26

The icon located at the bottom left of the menu allows you to preview only the current page.

Publish and Share Your Sound Online

Figures 5.27 through 5.30.

Figure 5.27

Preview window example.

Figure 5.28

A great way in which to share your work is to share your entire file online. Choose "File" from the top menu and select "Publish Online."

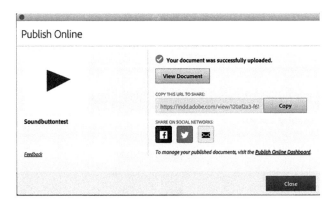

Figure 5.29

Once "Publish Online" is selected, select "View Document" or click "Copy" and then paste the link into a browser.

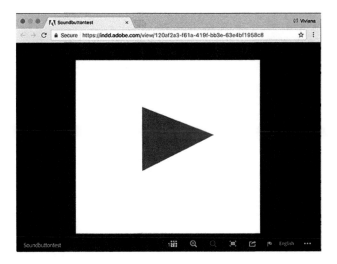

Figure 5.30

Document available online.

6

Video

In Adobe Premiere, videos can be professionally edited with many types of tools and a variety of options to export video files, from high quality to small versions for the web.

Video Libraries

1. Fotolia, part of Adobe, at https://www.fotolia.com/Info/Videos
2. Pexels Videos at https://videos.pexels.com/
3. Video Blocks at https://www.videoblocks.com/videos
4. Shutterstock at https://www.shutterstock.com/video/
5. Videvo at https://www.videvo.net/
6. Pixabay at https://pixabay.com/videos/
7. Makerbook at http://makerbook.net/video/
8. Video Cloud at https://pixabay.com/en/videos/cloud-sky-grey-clouds-cloudy-sky-9153/

Bringing Video Files into InDesign

The only video formats compatible with InDesign are .FLV, .F4V, .MP4, .MPEG, .AVI, .Quicktime, and .MOV. Furthermore, as mentioned in Chapter 5, InDesign allows audio files with the .MP3 extension.

Adobe Premiere

Figures 6.1 through 6.11.

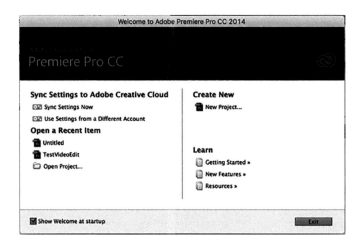

Figure 6.1

When the Premiere Pro CC application opens, you can open a past project from the history section on the left, under the title "Open a Recent Item," or you can create a new movie by selecting "New Project" under "Create New."

Figure 6.2

In the "New Project" window, give the project a name and location as well as set the display formats of the video and audio. Once the settings have been selected, click "OK."

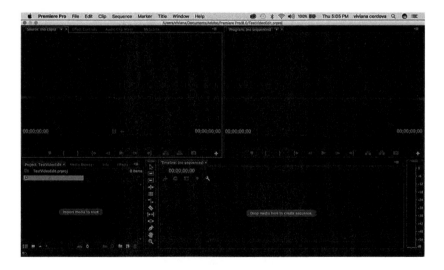

Figure 6.3

Adobe Premiere Pro user interface.

Figure 6.4

To bring video files to edit into Premiere, select "File" and "Import." Then, select a movie file from your computer and click "Import."

Figure 6.5

Once the video has been imported into Premiere, you can see it in the folder titled "Project: (Name of file here)," including the name of the file and the length.

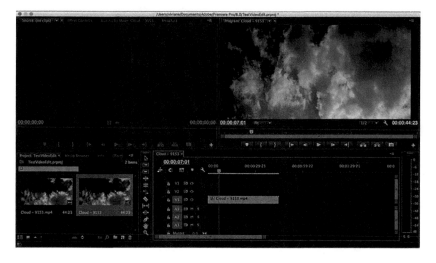

Figure 6.6

The gray outline at the bottom right shows where the videos and audio can be edited. The top right shows the video being edited.

Figure 6.7

Once you have edited the video file, go to "File," select "Export" and then "Media." A window titled "Export Settings" will appear.

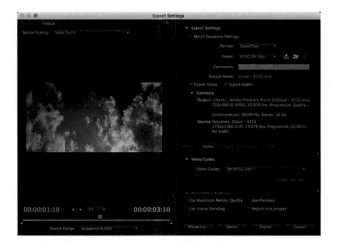

Figure 6.8

"Export Settings" provide many options for choosing the format of the video, choosing to export video and audio either alone or together, effects, video codec, audio options, and rendering quality. After making your choices, click "Export."

Figure 6.9

The options are Effects, Video, Audio, Captions, and FTP. In this example, "Video" is selected. Under Video Codec, MPEG-4 Video is selected from the drop-down menu.

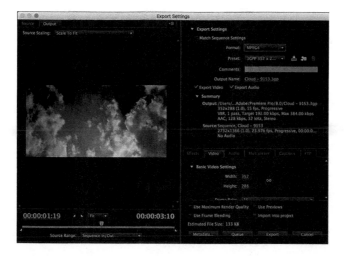

Figure 6.10

In this example, "Video" is selected. Under the Basic Video Settings, the width and height are being changed.

Figure 6.11

Once the export settings have been changed, click "Export" at the bottom-right corner. A window will ask you where you want to save your file. Then, the movie file will be ready for placement in InDesign.

iMovie

Figures 6.12 through 6.24.

Figure 6.12

With iMovie open, click "Create New."

Figure 6.13

Once you click "Create New," a small window offers two options: "Movie" and "Trailer." "Movie" provides a broader set of options with which to edit the video and "Trailer" provides a movie trailer template.

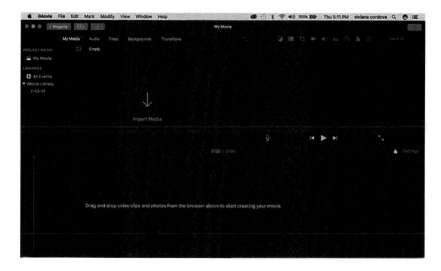

Figure 6.14

To start bringing in videos, drag and drop the movie files or photos to the bottom half of the iMovie interface.

Figure 6.15

Another option is to choose "File" and "Import Media."

Figure 6.16

Under "Import," select the desired file from your local directory and click "Import Selected."

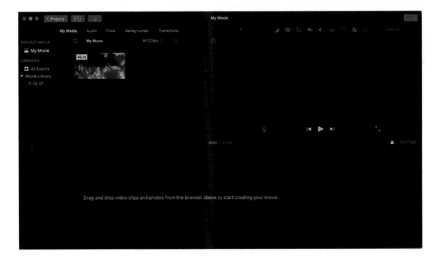

Figure 6.17

Once you have selected the movie, audio, or photo, it will show up in the iMovie interface at the top left. This example shows a video of a blue sky with clouds.

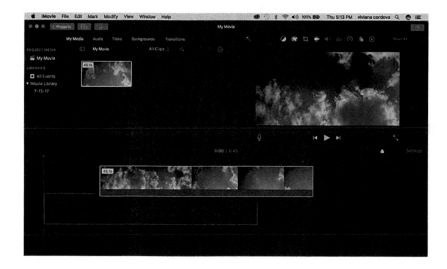

Figure 6.18

Now select that movie and drag it to the timeline at the bottom of the interface.

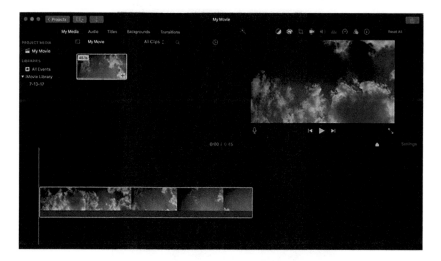

Figure 6.19

Once the movie is in the timeline, it can be edited. You can also bring more media to the timeline by following the instructions in Figures 6.15 through 6.18.

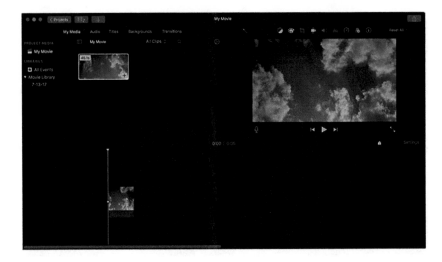

Figure 6.20

The movie is edited at the bottom of the interface. In Figure 6.19, the movie is very long (45 minutes). By dragging in the sides of the movie, the clip is reduced to five seconds.

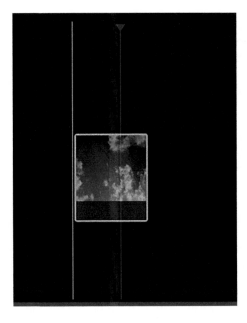

Figure 6.21

During editing, when you select a movie clip, it must be highlighted in blue to be edited.

Figure 6.22

At the top right of the iMovie interface are options to export the movie. Select "File."

Figure 6.23

Here, you have the option to choose various options from Format, Resolution, Quality, and Compress. Once you have made your decisions, click "Next."

Figure 6.24

Under "File," you can look through your files to select the right media for your project. Then select "Save."

Bringing Video Files into InDesign

Earlier, this chapter showed how to prepare video files in Adobe Premiere and iMovie once the right movie file has been exported. In InDesign, bringing in videos follows the same steps as those to bring in other media files (Chapters 3 through 5, Figures 6.25 through 6.32).

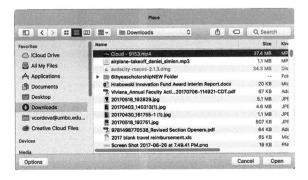

Figure 6.25

In InDesign, select "File" and "Place" or Command+D (Mac)/Windows+D (PC).

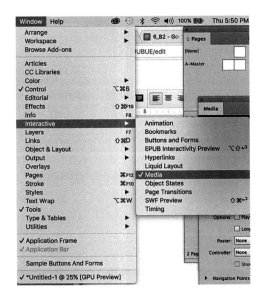

Figure 6.26

To see more information about any interactive media that have been imported into InDesign, click "Interactive" and "Media."

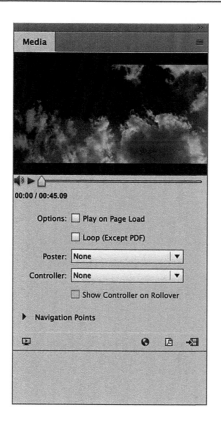

Figure 6.27

Selecting a movie or sound will provide information about the file. You can also edit options for the video: "Play on Page Load," "Loop," "Poster," "Controller," and "Navigation Points."

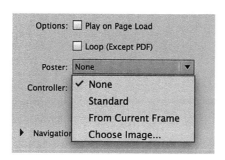

Figure 6.28

In the "Poster" option, you can select from four options in the drop-down menu: "None," "Standard," "From Current Frame," or "Choose Image."

Figure 6.29

The drop-down menu of the "Controller" option provides 18 options to for the appearance of the controller of the movie file.

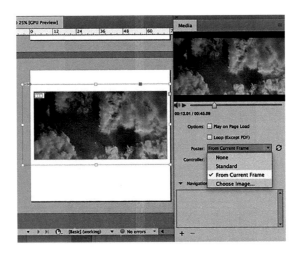

Figure 6.30

In the "Poster" option, the drop-down menu provides the options "None," "Standard," "From Current Frame" (selecting a section of the video at the top), and "Choose Image."

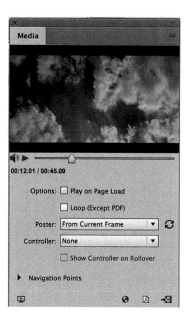

Figure 6.31

At bottom are four icons used for the following purposes: (1) the TV screen icon for previewing EPUB or choosing the "Click Spread SWF" option, (2) the world icon for bringing videos in from a URL, (3) the Acrobat icon for exporting to an interactive PDF, and (4) the film icon for placing a video or audio file.

Figure 6.32

The icon on the bottom left in the "Media Window" previews the current page. In this case, it is showing the movie placed on the page.

Bringing Video Files into InDesign

SECTION III
Recipes for Interactive Prototypes

7

Presentations

This section explains how to create an interactive PDF presentation by using the basic tools of interactive software such as links, buttons, pages, images, sounds, and videos. Presentations provide direct information to its audience, so they must be legible. Furthermore, the typeface and color used throughout the presentation should be consistent and clear with imagery, video, or audio provided as necessary.

When creating a presentation, the content should be concise and easy to understand. The type size should be at least 40 pt, although this will vary according to the amount of space and mode of presentation. A paragraph is sufficient to provide information in a presentation. It is better to keep the number of images or videos low (one or two) if you are trying to explain them. Make image backgrounds blurry using the blur tool in Photoshop, or create another level of hierarchy to create contrast and deliver the right message.

Document Setup

If you will be showing the presentation on a screen, select "Intent: Web" in "Document Setup." If you are printing the presentation, choose "Print," and the measurement will change to inches. If you plan to share the presentation digitally, keep in mind that the size is in pixels and the color is red, green, and blue (RGB) (Figure 7.1).

When setting up the pages and size for a presentation, it is necessary to use one page at a time, rather than a spread. Therefore, do not check the "Facing Pages" checkbox.

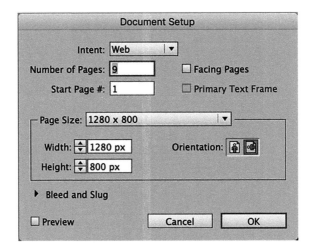

Figure 7.1

"Document Setup" window in InDesign.

Creating a Grid

Modular Grid

I encourage you to create a modular grid, which will help you nest images and text by aligning objects both vertically and horizontally, thus creating a more engaging design for the presentation (Figures 7.2 through 7.7).

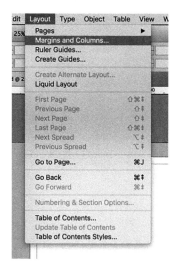

Figure 7.2

Choose "Layout" and then "Margins and Columns."

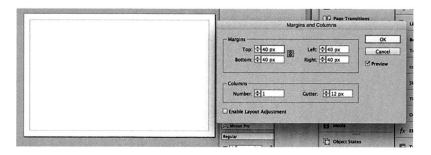

Figure 7.3

Set the values for "Margins and Columns" on the "Master" page located in the "Pages" section.

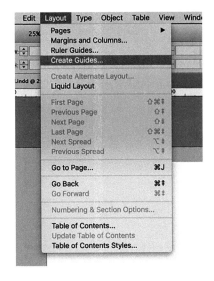

Figure 7.4

Choose "Layout" and "Create Guides."

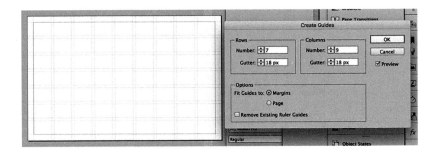

Figure 7.5

Set the values for the rows, columns, and gutter.

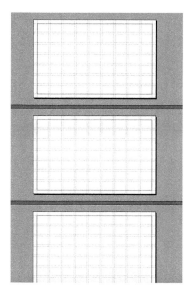

Figure 7.6

When creating a grid in the A-Master, the values set will automatically show on all the pages.

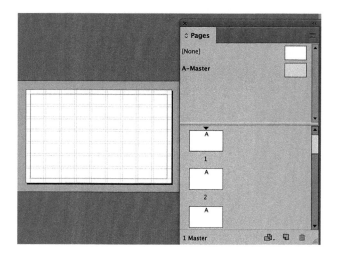

Figure 7.7

The A-Master and pages 1–3 are connected, because the letter "A" is located at the top of each page.

Column Grid

Figures 7.8 through 7.10.

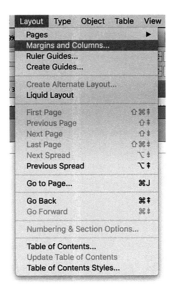

Figure 7.8

Choose "Layout" and then "Margins and Columns."

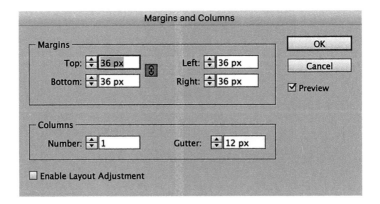

Figure 7.9

The "Margins and Columns" window.

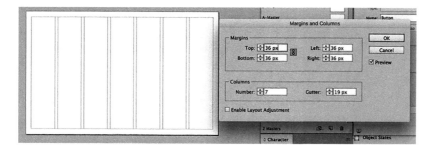

Figure 7.10

Setting the grid with only margins and columns limits the layout to vertical columns. If this is all you need, it is a good option.

Master Pages

Master pages provide structure for the design of the presentation; whatever you place on a master page will be repeated on all the other pages. You can also use more than one master page (Figures 7.11 through 7.14).

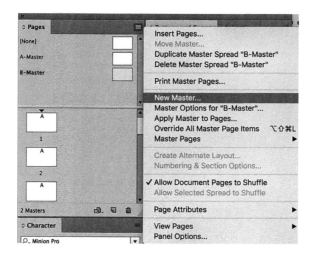

Figure 7.11

In the "Pages" window, select "New Master."

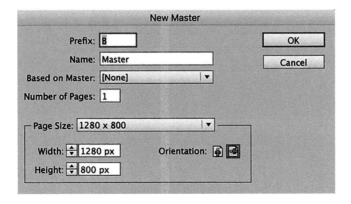

Figure 7.12

Set the values for the B-Master.

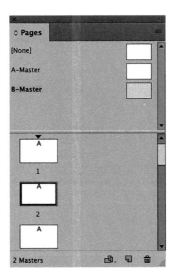

Figure 7.13

Select the new B-Master and drag the master page to any page (in this case, move the image to page 2). After dropping and releasing the mouse, the letter inside page 2, which is letter "A" as pictured earlier, will change to the letter "B."

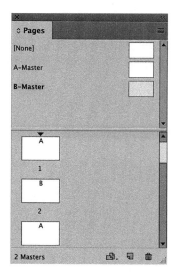

Page 2 is now using the B-Master.

Setting Pages in InDesign

When adding or removing pages, there are two main parts to the lower half of the Pages menu tool window. The top section is a menu for adding or deleting master pages. On master pages, you can place and organize the content. If you set a master page for a group of pages, you can add more than one master page by selecting "New Master" from the drop-down menu on the right in the window box (Figure 7.15).

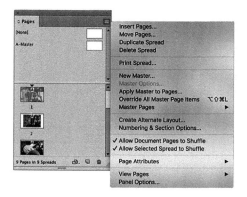

Figure 7.15

The top-right hamburger menu shows a drop-down menu.

Cover

The cover of the presentation should provide the title and the names of the authors/presenters. If possible, use color and/or an image:

Bringing Images into InDesign

This is one way to bring images into InDesign:

1. From the vertical icon toolbox, select the rectangular icon with an "x" inside, or press F. Go to the page to which you want to add the image. Once you have found the correct location, draw a rectangle and press Command+D (Mac) or Windows+D (PC). A window will pop up from where you can search for the image you are planning to place.

   Click on the relevant page, and press Command+D (Mac) or Windows+D (PC). Again, a window will pop up to search for the image. Once you have selected the image, the pointer of the mouse will automatically give you the rectangular shape option, with which you can draw a rectangle and place the image.

Preparing Images for Presentation

Spend time analyzing the images for use in the presentation. Do not just grab images and place them without ensuring consistent design. Take a few minutes to look at the sizes, resolutions, and the way in which the images are cropped and photographed. Find a way of organizing them by content, color, or form. If the images are too different or hard to organize and color is not important for the presentation, it might be better to make them black and white or monotone in Photoshop. This will also increase the readability of the text.

Ways to Organize Your Images

a. Full-screen image with caption.
b. Full-screen image without caption. The caption can be placed on the page before or after the page with the image.
c. Image taking one-third of the slide.
d. Image taking three-quarters of the slide.
e. Do not place an image halfway down the page. This breaks the design and creates two separate designs on one page. Always divide the grid of the content into at least thirds (as shown in the example that follows).
f. Image in the background.
g. More than one image.
h. Image as a cover for the presentation.

Layers

Selecting the "Layers" option from the "Window" menu allows you to create layers, and to hide and unhide them. You can also name the layers as you like. The image above the InDesign file has two layers: (1) background and (2) title. Layers allow you to organize the levels of hierarchy in the document. There is no limit to the number of layers you may create, but keep them orderly. If you no longer need a layer, click the trash icon to delete it (Figure 7.16).

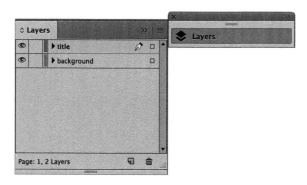

Figure 7.16

Layers toolbox.

Buttons

Presentations might need buttons to go backward or forward to the next page. If you need them, it is important to place them in a location that is not distracting to the viewer. Please see the following example (Figures 7.17 through 7.20).

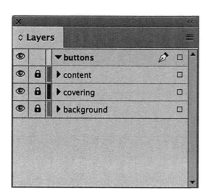

Figure 7.17

In the "Layers" window, create another level of layers. Ensure the new layer is placed above all the layers and name it "buttons," so you can recognize it.

Figure 7.18

Create a rectangular shape by using the rectangular tool located on the left side of the InDesign interface. Place this shape in another layer by itself.

Figure 7.19

Create two vector shapes that have the appearance of arrows.

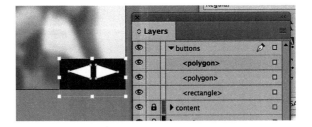

Figure 7.20

In the "Layers" window, where you created the "buttons" layer, clicking the arrow next to the "buttons" shows <polygon>, <polygon>, and <rectangle>. These shapes, selected on the left side, are for navigating this presentation. You decide on the colors and size.

Creating the Buttons

The "Buttons and Forms" window is only activated when you click an object that you are making into a button (shape, image, text). Once the object has been selected, you should be able to see "Type" activated, and you can then click on the drop-down menu arrow (Figures 7.21 through 7.24).

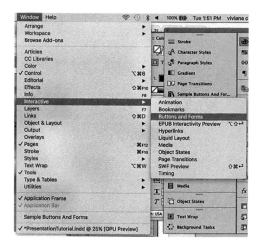

Figure 7.21

Go to Window > Interactive > Buttons and Forms.

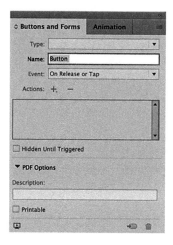

Figure 7.22

Name the button in the textbox next to "Name."

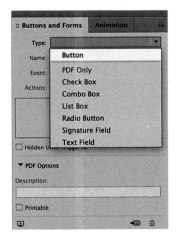

Figure 7.23

Select "Type" from the drop-down menu and choose "Button."

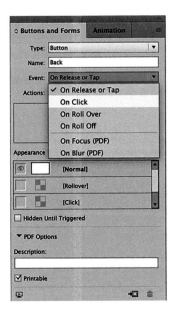

Figure 7.24

Give the new button a name by typing in the textbox next to "Name." In this example, the button is called "Back." The next option is "Event." Select this from the drop-down menu and choose "On Click."

The other "Event" options mean the following:

On Release or Tap: Use this option when viewing the presentation only through a touch-screen device.

On Click: Use when interacting with the presentation through a mouse or a touch pad.

On Roll Over: Chosen to make something happen when the user rolls over the button, without the need to tap or click.

On Roll Off: Activated when you move away from the button.

On Focus (PDF): This action only works when the user presses the button for a long period of time or presses the Tab key.

On Blur (PDF): This action works when the focus (see above) goes to another button or form.

When Objects Become Buttons

Figure 7.25.

Figure 7.25

When objects become buttons, it is easy to see the difference: The object will have dashed lines around it when selected in InDesign.

Actions

Select the button with the arrow pointing to the right and press + in the "Buttons and Forms" window shown in the following Figures 7.26 through 7.31.

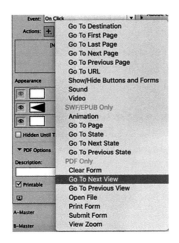

Figure 7.26

The "Actions" drop-down menu provides a wide range of options, but choose carefully. If you are making an interactive PDF, as in this example, you must only select from "PDF Only" and below.

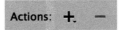

Figure 7.27

Only select from the "PDF Only" section: "Clear Form," "Go To Next View," "Go To Previous View," "Open File," "Print Form," "Submit Form," and "View Zoom."

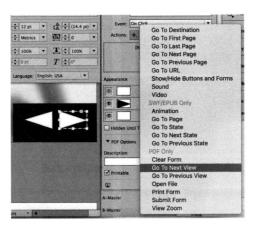

Figure 7.28

Choose "Go To Next View."

Figure 7.29

Repeat for the other arrow pointing left, and select "Go To Previous View."

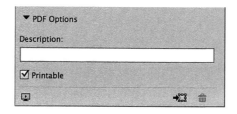

Figure 7.30

"Buttons and Forms" has a section called "Appearance" (located below "Actions") that provides three options allowing control over the appearance of the object in three stages: Normal, Rollover, and Click. In the above-mentioned example, the appearance changes from white to black on Rollover. Select the buttons you want to change and then click "Rollover." The shape you want to change is selected. Then, go to "Color" and change it from white to black.

Figure 7.31

Toward the bottom of the "Buttons and Forms" window is "PDF Options," where you can add information that may help to the "Description" section. You can also check the "Printable" checkbox if you want the PDF to be printable.

Setting Type

The Character tool provides many important options. Do not just leave the text in Times New Roman; give it a personality. In the above-mentioned case, the typeface selected is Verdana, the weight is bold, and the size is 33 pt. The space between the sentences is 48 pt. The aligning is using "Metrics," but another choice is "Optical" alignment (Figures 7.32 and 7.33).

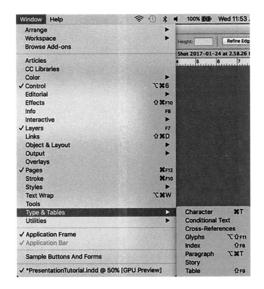

Figure 7.32

From the top menu of "Window," select "Type & Tables" and "Character." Then, return to "Type & Tables" and select "Paragraph."

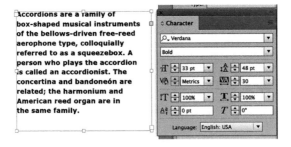

Figure 7.33

In the previous image, there is a column in a textbox and the "Character" window is on the right. When the content is highlighted inside the textbox, it is easy to make changes by using the Character tool.

The spacing between the characters is 30. Try to keep the proportion of the height and width of the letterforms to 100%, because typeface designers spend a long time drawing the letterforms. They do not want the anatomy of each character to be disfigured, so changing their proportions would be a disastrous decision. Keep the letterforms as they were created. The last two options allow moving specific letterforms above the baseline to make them close to superscript. The last option on the right slants letterforms, which is not recommended for the reasons explained earlier (i.e., to keep the letterforms proportional to how they were created) (Figure 7.34).

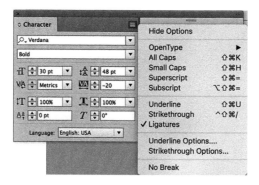

Figure 7.34

On the top right of the menu is a hamburger icon. When you click on it, the menu comes out on the right side, as shown earlier. This option gives you more ways in which to create a hierarchy. The "Open Type" option gives you a wide variety of font families, such as swashes and fractions. The other options are self-explanatory: "All Caps," "Small Caps," "Superscript," "Subscript," "Underline," "Strikethrough," "Ligatures," "Underline Options," "Strikethrough Options," and "No Break" (selecting a word at which you do not want a break will automatically move it up a line).

Learning to Apply Character and Paragraph Style

Figures 7.35 and 7.36.

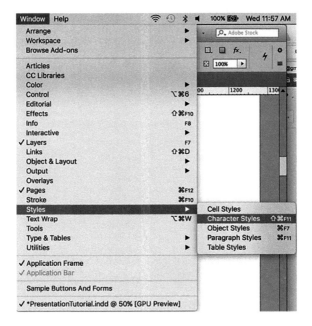

Figure 7.35

From "Window," select "Styles" and then "Character Styles" or "Paragraph Styles."

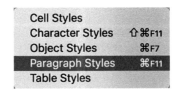

Figure 7.36

Close-up of the options in "Styles."

Page Transitions

Figures 7.37 through 7.41.

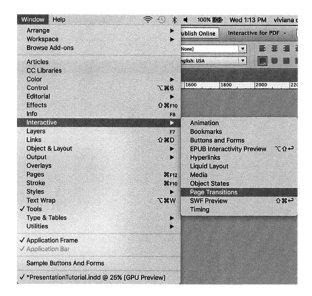

Figure 7.37

Go to "Window" and then select "Interactive" and "Page Transitions."

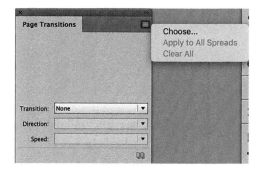

Figure 7.38

In "Page Transitions," select "Choose" at the top right.

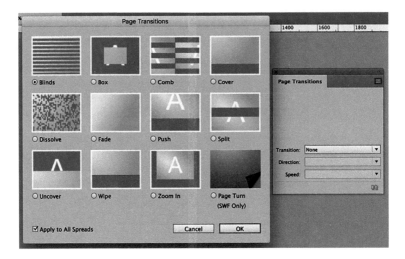

Figure 7.39

This window provides a wide range of options for transitions on all pages or on specific pages. The checkbox at the bottom left applies the transition to all spreads. If you uncheck this box, only the page on which you are working will have a transition.

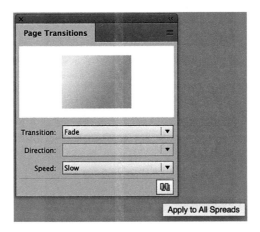

Figure 7.40

After selecting "Fade" from the previous window, the "Page Transitions" window shows "Fade" with three "Speed" options: Slow, Medium, and Fast. On the bottom right, you can again click on the icon to make the transition from page to page apply to all pages.

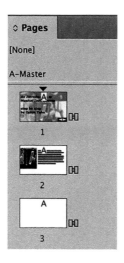

Figure 7.41

After the transition has been applied, go to the "Pages" window. The small icon at the bottom right of each page confirms that the transition has been applied to all pages.

Animations

Bringing Many Images onto a Page at Once

If you are on an InDesign page and want to bring in many images, click on the page and hold the keys Command+D (Mac) or Windows+D (PC). These keys place an image in InDesign (Figures 7.42 through 7.50).

Figure 7.42

Place window pop-up.

Figure 7.43

Select the images you want to bring into InDesign. In this case, six images are selected.

Figure 7.44

The cursor automatically brings the images onto the page when you start creating a rectangle or square. As you create the shape, press the right and up arrow keys at the same time. Dashed lines appear, creating a grid, and you will start to see the images.

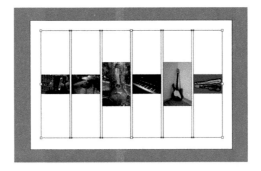

Figure 7.45

As the images are of different sizes, only a vertical grid is created, with the images aligned along the center. If you have several equally sized images, for example, they will line up in vertical and horizontal rows.

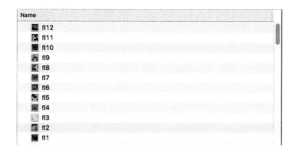

Figure 7.46

Using Command+D (Mac) or Windows+D (PC) lists the images.

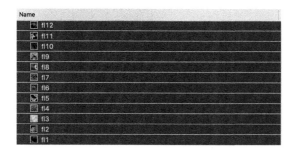

Figure 7.47

Select the required images.

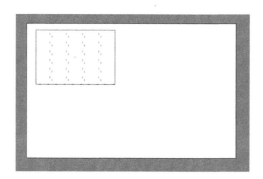

Figure 7.48

Create a rectangle by pressing down the right arrows at the same time.

Figure 7.49

Pressing the up and right arrows helps divide the images evenly, both horizontally and vertically.

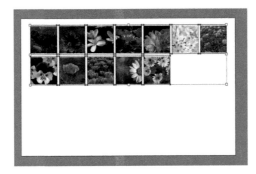

Figure 7.50

Here, all images are sized the same and placed in the rectangle at once.

Saving a File as a PDF (Interactive)

To save a PDF version of a file, first go to "File" in the main menu and then select "Export" from the drop-down menu. At the bottom, select "PDF (Interactive)." For further information, Chapter 12 has a step-by-step export tutorial.

8

Forms

This chapter provides step-by-step guidance for how to create an interactive PDF form with check and submit buttons, content boxes, tabs, and typography. Forms are not usually something that users choose to interact with but rather present a necessary task. Therefore, forms should be organized and easy to read, with plenty of space.

Over time, forms have become more digitalized. Hence, they need to be more innovatively designed so users will have pleasant experiences when filling them out. Please follow these rules:

1. Do not overwhelm the user.
2. Do not overlap the text.
3. Do not use text smaller than 12 pt or 12 px.
4. Always use character spacing in all contents.
5. Use leading spacing between lines of text, buttons, boxes, and any form fields.
6. Do not place too much content on the page (test with users).
7. Always ask for extra feedback from future users.

Creating a Basic Form in InDesign

Figures 8.1 through 8.43.

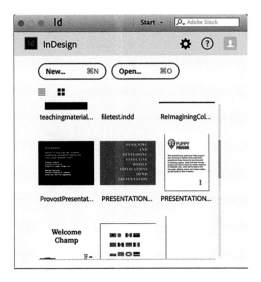

Figure 8.1

Create a new document by clicking the "New" button. The "Open" button opens a file created previously.

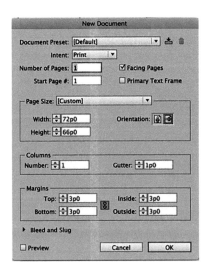

Figure 8.2

After clicking "New," a window will appear titled "New Document."

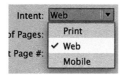

Figure 8.3

In the "Intent" section, select whether you want a document for print, web, or mobile. These options provide predetermined sizes.

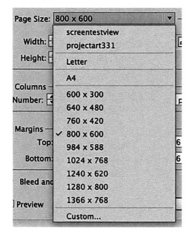

Figure 8.4

Choosing "Web" provides a wide range of options for different screen sizes.

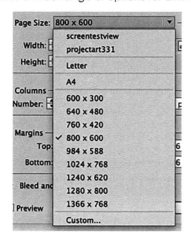

Figure 8.5

Preset sizes will appear at the top. In this case, they are called "screentestview" and "projectart331."

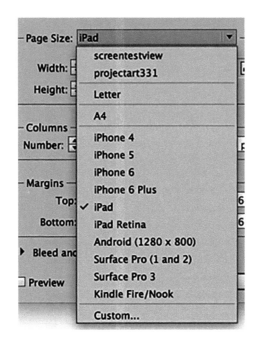

Figure 8.6

Choosing "Mobile" provides a wide range of options for mobile screens.

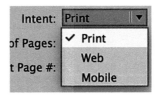

Figure 8.7

Choosing "Print" provides a wide range of options for print.

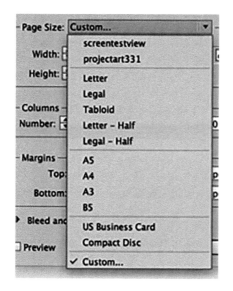

Figure 8.8

There is also a custom option here, as well.

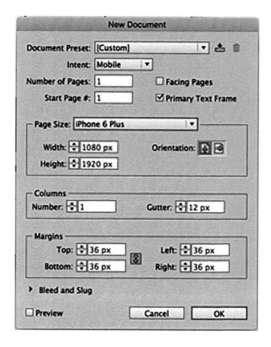

Figure 8.9

In this example, the Intent is "Mobile" and the page size is "iPhone 6 Plus."

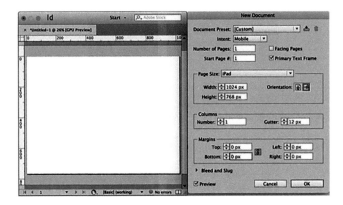

Figure 8.10

If you check the bottom-left option of "Preview," you can see the document while choosing the right size for it. You also have options to set document orientation (horizontal or vertical), columns, and margins.

Figure 8.11

You can always return to change the document size by choosing "File" and selecting "Document Setup" from the top-left menu.

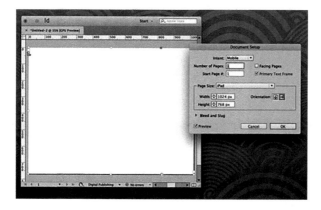

Figure 8.12

The "Document Setup" window will appear, where you can edit the following: "Intent," "Number of Pages," "Start Page," "Page Size," "Width," "Height," "Orientation," and "Bleed and Slug."

Figure 8.13

If you want to save the file as a copy, go to the top-left menu. Then, select "File" and "Save As."

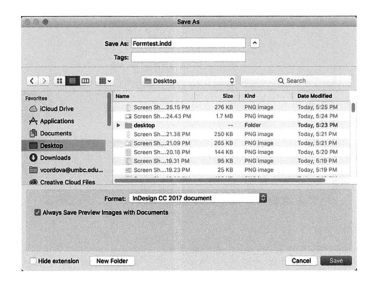

Figure 8.14

Here you have the option to change the format, as well.

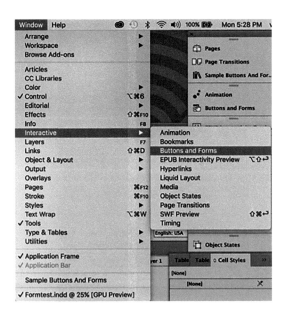

Figure 8.15

To set up the "Form Workspace," go to "Window" and select "Interactive." From there, select "Buttons and Forms."

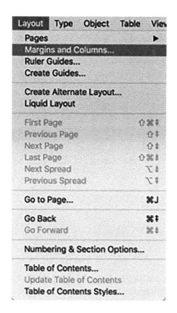

Figure 8.16

To edit or add margins and columns, go to the top menu and select "Layout." Under the drop-down menu, select "Margins and Columns."

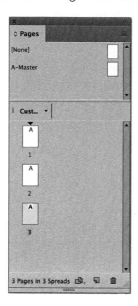

Figure 8.17

The "Pages" window can be accessed from the top menu by selecting "Window" > "Pages."

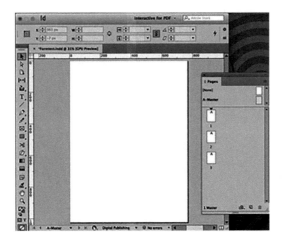

Figure 8.18

"Pages" is divided into two sections. First, there is a Master section where you can add more master pages to make the pages consistent. In the second part, you can see the master pages in action. If a master page is assigned to a page, there is a small letter at the top of each page. In this example, there are three pages. Only the A-Master is assigned to all three pages, because there is an "A" on each page. Only one master page can be assigned per page.

Figure 8.19

To create a modular grid to ensure a consistent layout, select "Layout" from the top menu and then "Create Guides."

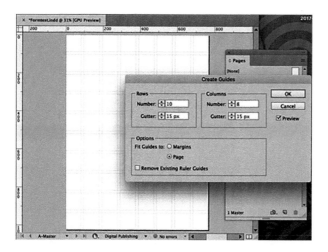

Figure 8.20

In "Create Guides," you have the option to create a grid and set a gutter (the space between the columns and rows). If you create a grid, do so on a master page, so the grid will be activated on all pages associated with that master.

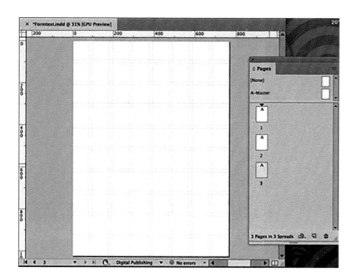

Figure 8.21

A modular grid created with vertical and horizontal light lines on page 3.

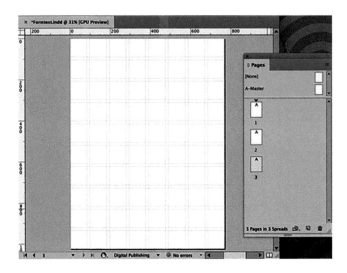

Figure 8.22

To check that the grid has been applied to all three pages in this case, click twice on each page in the "Pages" window. As mentioned earlier in this chapter, make sure the guides were created in the A-Master so that each page shares the same structural guides.

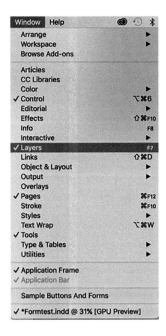

Figure 8.23

Layers are activated by going to the top menu and selecting "Window" > "Layers."

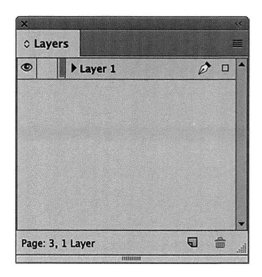

Figure 8.24

The "Layers" window activates the layers for the document.

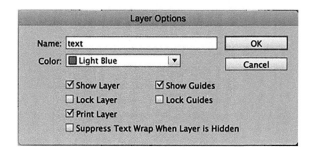

Figure 8.25

If you click on any of the layers twice, you can edit that layer. The options include "Show Layer," "Lock Layer," "Print Layer," "Suppress Text Wrap When Layer is Hidden," "Show Guides," and "Lock Guides."

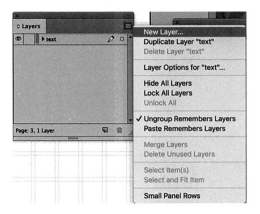

Figure 8.26

In "Layers," the hamburger menu at the top right also provides other options, such as "New Layer."

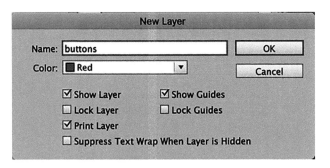

Figure 8.27

If you click "New Layer," you can give the layer a name and set your desired settings.

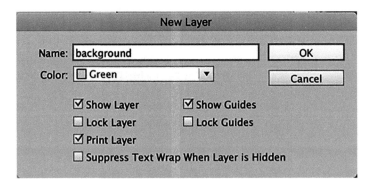

Figure 8.28

You can also change the color of the layer's label.

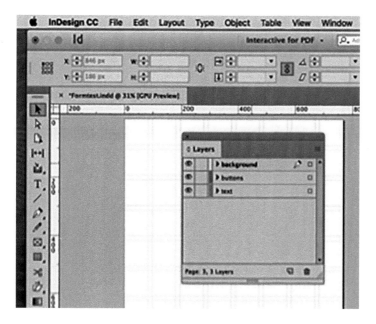

Figure 8.29

In the "Layers" window, each layer has a differently colored bar on the left side. If it has been edited, there is a small ink pen icon on the right side of the layer.

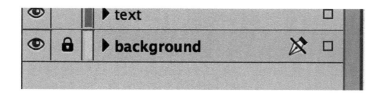

Figure 8.30

To lock the layer, click on the lock icon next to the eye icon for each layer. In this case, the "background" layer is locked, as shown by the lock icon to the left. Furthermore, on the right side, the pen ink icon with a line through it confirms that the background layer is not usable or editable at this time. This layer can be reactivated by unlocking the layer's lock icon.

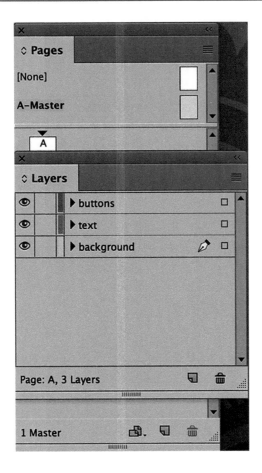

Figure 8.31

In the "Layers" window, three layers have already been created: "background," "buttons," and "text." You can add more layers by clicking on the page icon next to the trash can icon.

Figure 8.32

The tools section.

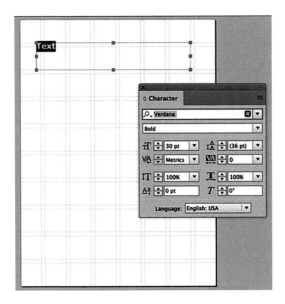

Figure 8.33

From the "Tools" window on the left side, choose the text tool. Click and drag to create a rectangle or square box. Then you can type inside the created textbox, as shown earlier. To activate the "Character" menu, go to the top menu and select "Window," then "Type & Tables." From the submenu, select "Character." The shortcut is Command+T (Mac) and Windows+T (PC).

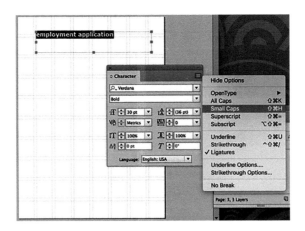

Figure 8.34

In the "Character" window, a menu appears after clicking the hamburger icon. At the top right, select "Small Caps." This option allows the text to have small caps (Make sure all characters are in lower case).

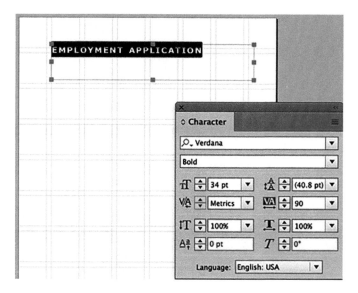

Figure 8.35

There are a wide variety of options in the "Character" window, such as type size, line height, kerning, alignment metrics, and optical alignment.

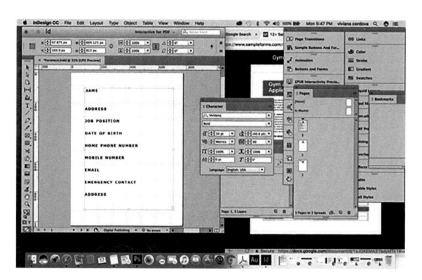

Figure 8.36

The textbox can easily be extended to add more text. In the above-mentioned image, a form list has been created.

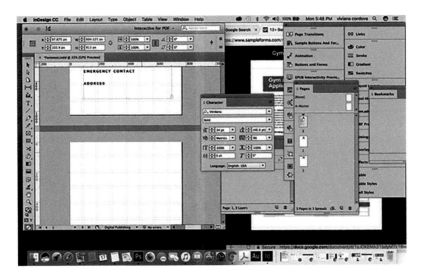

Figure 8.37

Also, the textbox can be extended into the next pages.

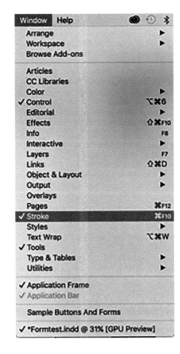

Figure 8.38

From the top menu, select "Window" and "Stroke" to create lines.

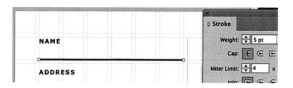

Figure 8.39

Make sure the stroke is long enough so the user is able to fit all the characters necessary to fit in the line.

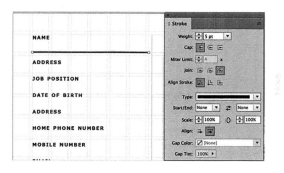

Figure 8.40

In this example, the stroke is five points. You can adjust the stroke through the various options, such as "Cap," "Join," "Align Stroke," and "Type."

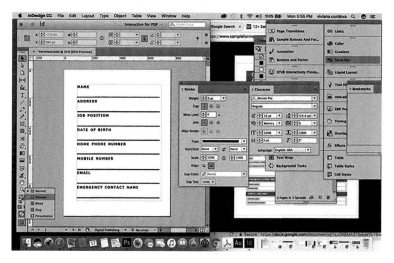

Figure 8.41

In this example, each title has a stroke below each line of text, creating a line that marks space where the user can enter his or her information. Using a larger type size is crucial to improve legibility. In addition, give enough space in each section; note the user-provided information can vary from user to user in terms of the numbers of characters.

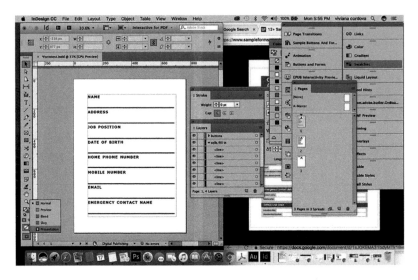

Figure 8.42

In the toolbox on the left, the last icon is a gray box. If you click and hold the cursor, the pop-up window provides the following options: "Normal," "Preview," "Bleed," "Slug," and "Presentation." In the above-mentioned image, the cursor is hovering on the option "Presentation."

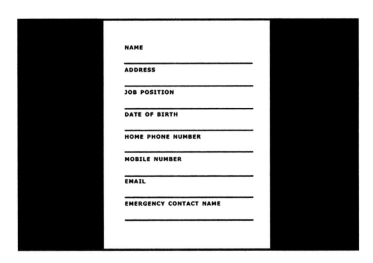

Figure 8.43

The "Presentation" preview removes everything from the screen, showing only the pages on which you are working, without guides or anything that might distract the viewer. This option allows users to revise any mistakes.

Types of Tools in Forms and How to Apply Them to an Interactive PDF

How to Create a Checkbox?

Figures 8.44 through 8.51.

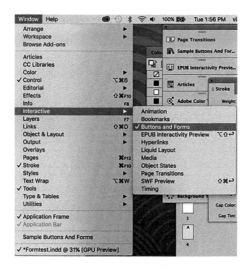

Figure 8.44

From the top menu, select "Window" > "Interactive." These options are essential to create a successful interactive piece in InDesign. In this case, we have selected "Buttons and Forms."

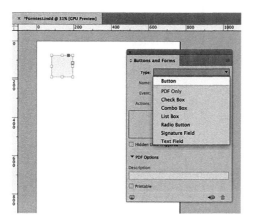

Figure 8.45

Create a square by using the shape tool and click on the created shape. To start editing the "Buttons and Forms" inside the window, click "Type." From the list of options, select "Check Box."

Figure 8.46

When a checkbox is created, a dashed blue outline will be added around the box. In the "Appearance" section, many options help you set the checkbox. In this example, "Normal On" and "Normal Off" are both checked on.

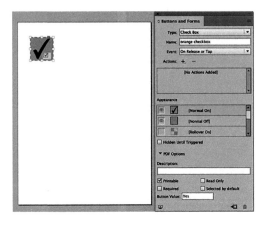

Figure 8.47

To test the checkbox, select "File" > "Export."

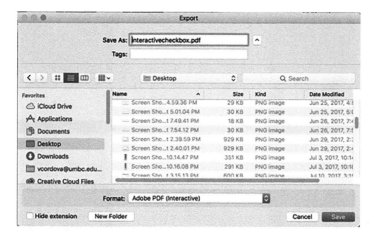

Figure 8.48

In the "Export" window, type the name of the PDF file you want to create and select the correct folder. Click "Save."

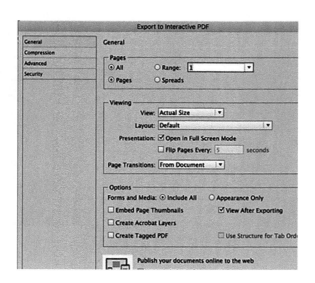

Figure 8.49

Then, an "Export to Interactive PDF" window will appear. In this example, I have selected "All Pages" and then clicked "Export." If you check on "View After Exporting" in the "Options" menu, the PDF file will open automatically after you click "Export."

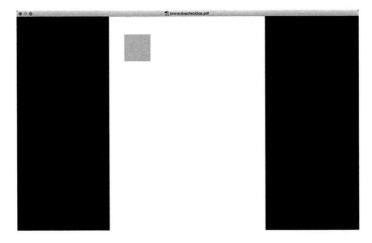

Figure 8.50

The PDF checkbox test opens automatically after exporting the file.

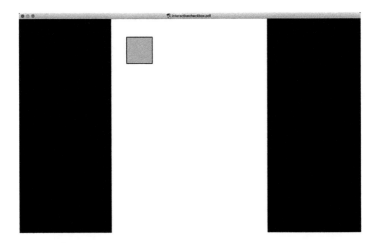

Figure 8.51

When you hover over the checkbox, a thin outline appears.

How to Create a Text Field?

Figures 8.52 through 8.60.

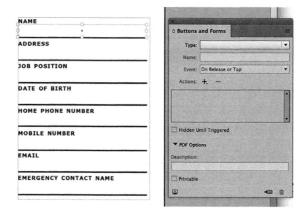

Figure 8.52

By using the toolbox on the left side, create a rectangular shape. The light gray outline box highlighted in the figure shows where the text field will be created. Once highlighted in the "Buttons and Forms" window on the right side, click "Type" to show the drop-down menu.

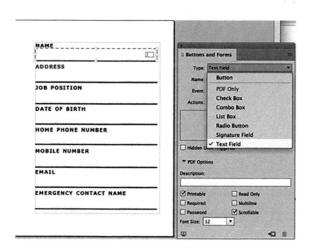

Figure 8.53

Select "Text Field" from the drop-down menu.

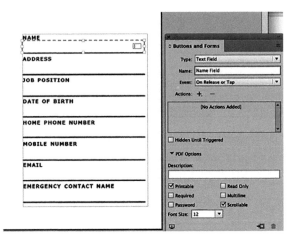

Figure 8.54

After selecting the "Text Field" option, the dashed gray outline can be copied and pasted onto the other lines to create more text fields.

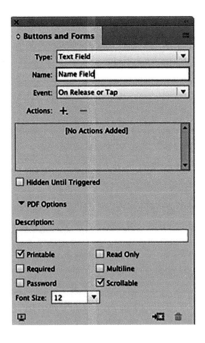

Figure 8.55

In the "Buttons and Forms" window, give the field a "Name" and "Event." In the section titled "PDF Options," you can choose whether you want any of the following: "Printable," "Required," "Password," "Read Only," "Multiline," and "Scrollable." You can also set the Text Field's "Font Size."

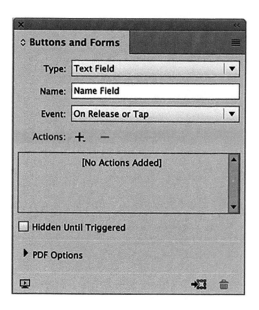

Figure 8.56

If you are not saving this project as a PDF file, please disregard the "PDF Options."

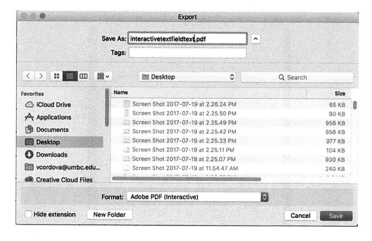

Figure 8.57

To test the file, go to the top menu and select "File" and "Export." Name the PDF file being exported and save it in the folder of your choice. In the "Format" section, choose "Adobe PDF (Interactive)" and click "Save."

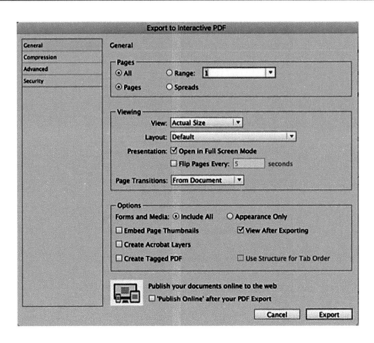

Figure 8.58

A window titled "Export to Interactive PDF" will pop up. Select "Export."

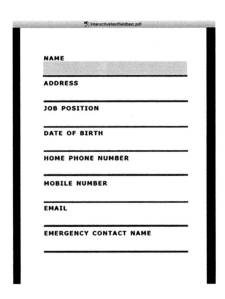

Figure 8.59

If you checked "View After Exporting" in the previous window, the PDF file will automatically open.

Figure 8.60

I typed my name in the text field under "Name." That text field in the form has now been filled.

How to Create a Combo Box?

Figures 8.61 through 8.71.

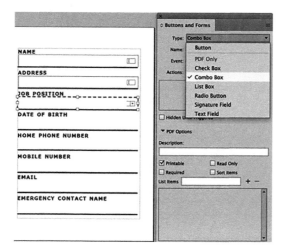

Figure 8.61

In the "Job Position" section of the document, create a rectangle. In "Button and Forms," select "Combo Box." Once selected, a dashed light gray line will appear around the rectangle where the Combo Box has been created.

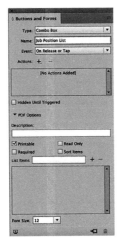

Figure 8.62

Once "Combo Box" has been selected, give it a name. In this example, the name is "Job Position List."

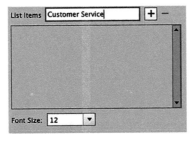

Figure 8.63

Toward the bottom, there is a section titled "List Items." In the text box, type the list options you want in the combo box. In this figure, "Customer Service" has been added. Then, click "+."

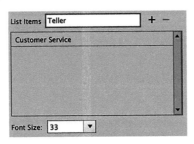

Figure 8.64

"Customer Service" has been created after clicking the "+" icon. The next option to add is "Teller."

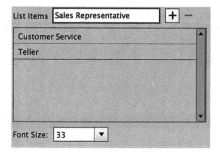

Figure 8.65

A third option has been created in the list, "Sales Representative."

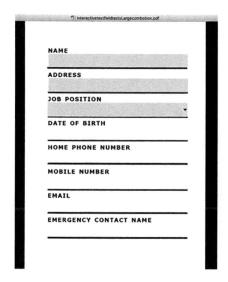

Figure 8.66

Export the PDF. For more information, see Figures 8.59 through 8.61.

Figure 8.67

The combo box appears in the PDF with a black arrow at the far right of the drop-down menu.

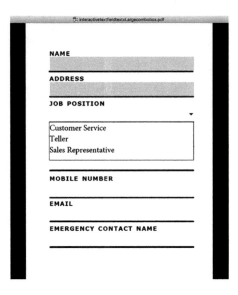

Figure 8.68

After clicking the drop-down menu, the three options are created as mentioned earlier in InDesign appear.

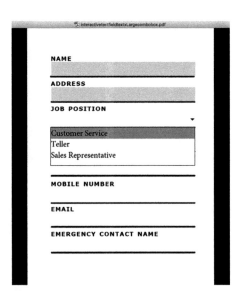

Figure 8.69

"Customer Service" selected in the above-mentioned example.

8. Forms

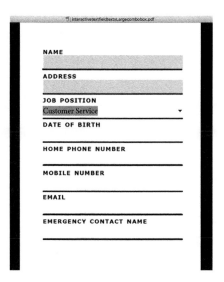

Figure 8.70

"Customer Service" chosen from the combo box.

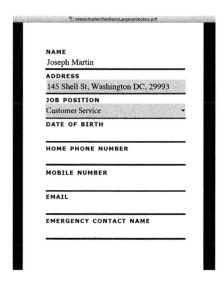

Figure 8.71

Name, Address, and Job Position are active, because the text fields and combo box for these fields were created in InDesign.

How to Create a List Box?

Figures 8.72 through 8.77.

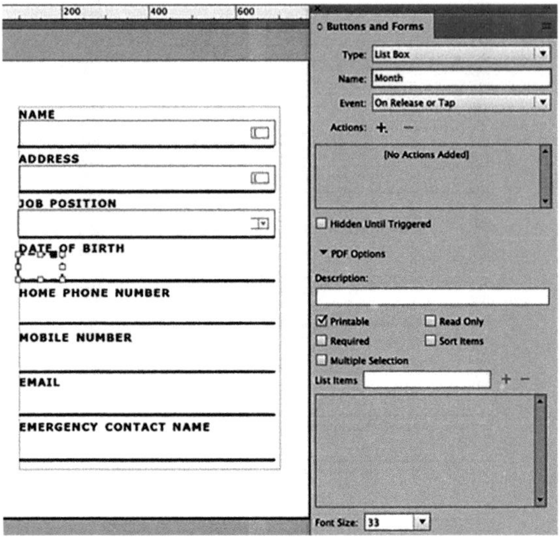

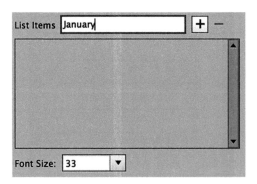

Figure 8.72

Create a rectangle below "Date of Birth." From "Buttons and Forms," select "List Box" in the "Type" section. Once the list box has been activated, it will have a dashed gray line around the rectangle.

Figure 8.73

In "Buttons and Forms," a section will appear titled "List Items." Start typing the list options in the text box. In the example, "January" has been typed. Clicking the "+" icon will add this item to the list.

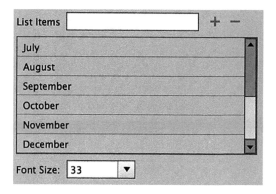

Figure 8.74

In this example, a 12-month calendar has been added to the list. The order will appear from top to bottom.

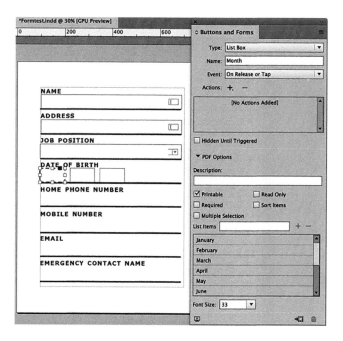

Figure 8.75

In the "Date of Birth" section, we need three rectangles, one each for Month, Date, and Year. Therefore, in this figure, three list boxes have been created.

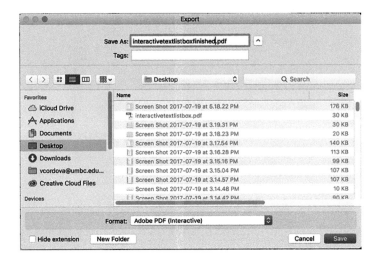

Figure 8.76

Export the PDF to test. For more information, see Figures 8.61 through 8.63.

Figure 8.77

In the PDF file, Month, Date and Year are activated. For Year, the list box is clearly visible because of the scroll activated in the figure.

How to Create a Radio Button?

Figures 8.78 and 8.79.

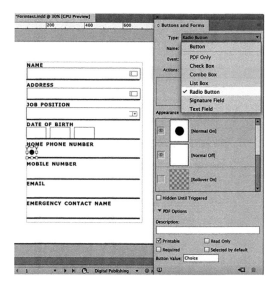

Figure 8.78

Create a rectangle by using the rectangle tool from the toolbox on the left side of InDesign. In the Type section of the "Buttons and Forms" window, select "Radio Button." In the "Appearance" section, select On and Off. The rectangle on the left will automatically have a radio button.

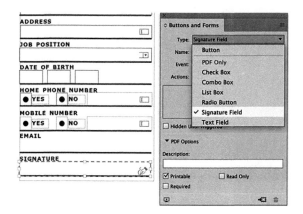

Figure 8.79

Under the labels "Home Phone Number" and "Mobile Number" are four radio buttons. In InDesign, these look like filled in, black circles. However, in the PDF, the user can turn them on and off.

How to Create a Signature Field?

Figures 8.80 through 8.84.

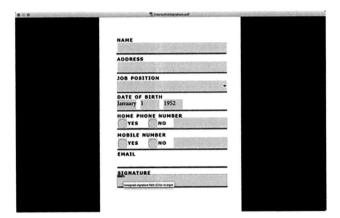

Figure 8.80

Below the text "Signature," create a rectangle of the size where the signature will go. In "Buttons and Forms" under the "Type" option, select "Signature Field." A dashed light gray line will be activated around the rectangle to confirm the "Signature Field" has been created.

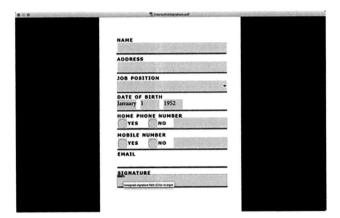

Figure 8.81

Export the PDF. For more information, see Figures 8.61 through 8.63. In the PDF file, the "Signature" section has a red tag at the top of the field and a yellow label that says, "Unsigned signature field (Click to sign)." In addition, the radio buttons in "Home Phone Numbers" and "Mobile Numbers" offer the choice of "YES" or "NO." Figure 8.79 shows the radio buttons at work.

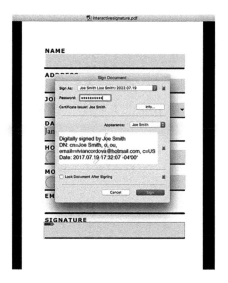

Figure 8.82

In the pop-up window titled "Sign Document," the user can choose from a signature already created in Acrobat or can create an entirely new signature in the "Appearance" section. After choosing the right signature, the user types in their password and clicks "Sign." An extra option, "Lock Document After Signing," means that nothing can be changed in the document after signing.

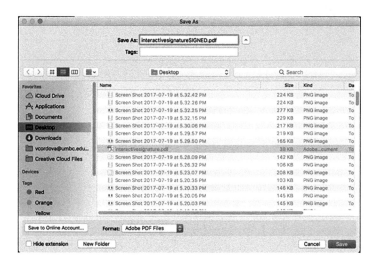

Figure 8.83

Give a name to the PDF file and save it in the right folder.

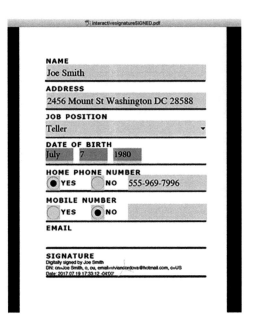

Figure 8.84

After opening the PDF file, the "Signature" section has a digital signature stamped with the time and date.

9

Magazines and Books

Interactive magazines and books are in high demand and can be accessed via devices such as tablets, phones, and desktops. Mobile app supports are not consistent throughout all digital publishing avenues. Therefore, when you are creating a magazine, you need to know from the beginning where you are going to publish it, for example, in Apple or Android app stores, an online store, or a website. Whatever you decide, you will need to consider restrictions in size, images, sound, video, and anything else they require. If you follow the rules, you will be able to create a satisfying product in a faster and more effective way. There is a wide variety of options when exporting files, and you will be able to access detailed information about the different types of exports in Chapter 12.

Some online companies will provide an InDesign template that you can download prior to starting the project, which can be very helpful as this will enable you to create your magazine according to their guidelines. Any misspellings in the figures of this chapter are intentional and part of the work in progress in the InDesign file.

Setting Up

Figures 9.1 through 9.12.

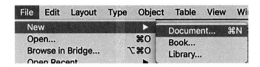

Figure 9.1

Creating a New Document.

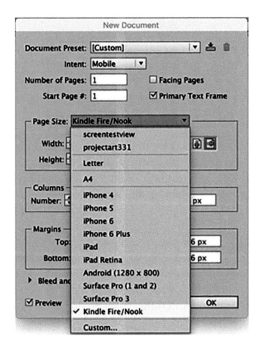

Figure 9.2

Once in the "New Document" box, choose "Page Size" from the drop-down menu.

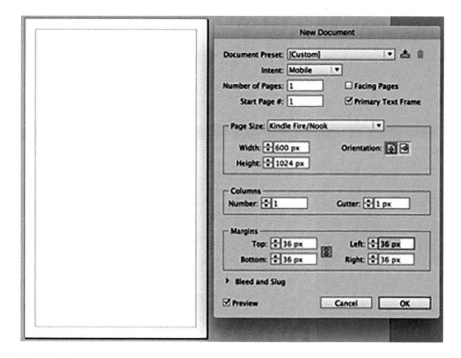

Figure 9.3

In "New Document," it will be helpful to set columns and margins if needed. In the bottom-left corner, there is a "Preview" checkbox. When the checkbox is checked, the Document being created can be seen at the same time, which can be very helpful when setting the New Document.

Figure 9.4

Choose "Window" from the top menu and then select "Workspace," and from the drop-down menu, click "Digital Publishing."

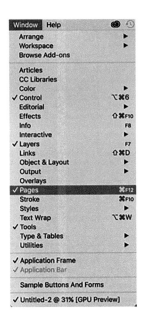

Figure 9.5

Select "Window" from the top menu and then choose "Pages."

Figure 9.6

The "Pages" window will open.

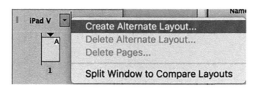

Figure 9.7

The Vertical icon page has a title at the top ("iPad V"), and next to it there is an arrow, which when clicked will cause a menu to appear. From this menu, select "Create Alternate Layout."

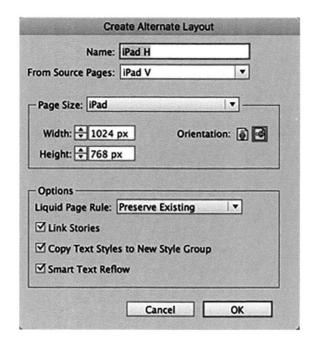

Figure 9.8

A new window will pop up and there you can create an alternate layout (in this example, a horizontal layout).

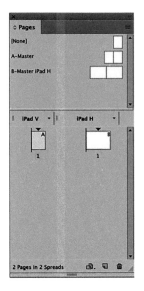

Figure 9.9

In this image, iPad V and iPad H were created. To add pages simply click the page icon at the bottom right next to the trash can icon. Every time the page icon is clicked, a new page will be added to the document.

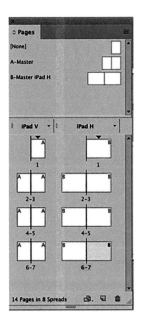

Figure 9.10

There is a creation of seven pages for each layout (vertical and horizontal).

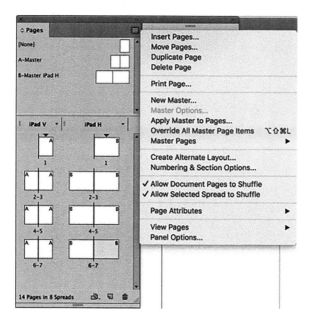

Figure 9.11

The top hamburger menu opens a list that allows many options, including Move pages and Insert pages.

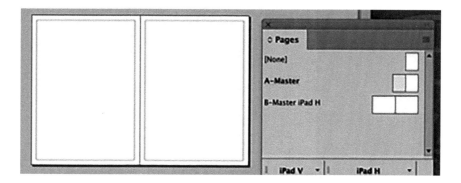

Figure 9.12

The top section of the "Pages" window is where the Master pages can be found. The Master pages are the structure for the rest of the pages.

Setting Up Grids

Figures 9.13 through 9.16.

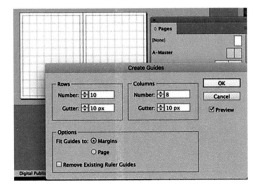

Figure 9.13

Create guides by choosing "Layout" from the top menu and then selecting "Create Guides." A window will pop up, allowing you to edit Rows and Columns. If the "Preview" checkbox is checked, you can easily see the changes live in the Master page. Once you are done, click "OK."

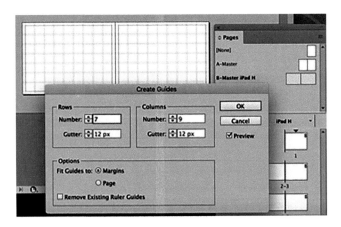

Figure 9.14

Repeat the previous method for the Horizontal layout as well. Obviously, it will be slightly different because the document is wider.

Figure 9.15

To save your document, go to "File" in the top menu and select "Save As."

Figure 9.16

In the "Save As" window, give your file a name. In the "Format" section, select InDesign CC 2017 document (This is the correct one). Choose InDesign CC 2017 template (to create consistency with other documents) or InDesign CS4 or later (IDML) (This file type allows you to open the file with other InDesign versions). When finished, click "Save."

Images

There is no need to use large resolution images. First, make sure the images are in pixels and set the resolution to between 72 ppi (pixels per inch) and 150 ppi. Do not use larger images because it is not necessary.

Some magazines are more richly interactive, providing videos, animations, and sound, for instance, especially when they are designed for apps. For more information, see Chapters 11 and 12. In the current example, however, our type of magazine needs an environment that is simple and easy to access from any device, and therefore the file size and the media need to be simple and easy to access.

Cover

Creating a Vertical Cover

The cover should be formatted according to the guidelines of the intended reading device. It is essential to know the size and the extra icons needed to be promoted in the specific app stores. So, when creating the prototype of the magazine, the user could have the closest version to the final version.

Readers will always gravitate to the cover because that is the only thing they see before buying the magazine. As such, it is necessary to design the artwork of the cover well, and most of all ensure that grabs the attention of the reader compared to the competitors in the marketplace.

For more information on how to import images into InDesign and Photoshop, see Chapter 3.

Making Changes to the Document after Creating the Files
Figures 9.17 and 9.18.

Figure 9.17

If you want to make changes to the size or number of pages, or rearrange the canvas (vertical or horizontal), then go to the top menu and select "File." From the menu, choose "Document Setup."

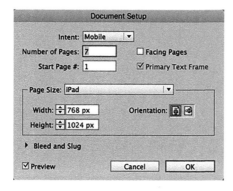

Figure 9.18

A window titled "Document Setup" will pop up. From there, you can make the necessary changes in size, orientation (horizontal or vertical), or even turn "Facing Pages" on or off.

Creating Layers

Figure 9.19.

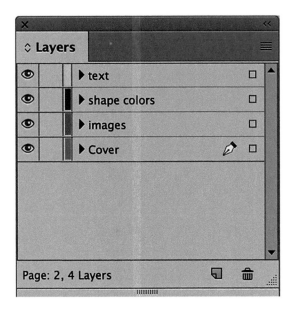

Figure 9.19

To work with layers, go to the "Window" menu at the top and then select "Layers," which will cause a new window to pop up. Creating various layers will help you keep your file organized. In this case, I created four layers: text, shape colors, images, and cover.

Creating a Horizontal Cover

Figures 9.20 through 9.27.

Figure 9.20

The cover in the above-mentioned example is already on page 1 in iPad V and now it is necessary to create a horizontal version of the cover. Click the arrow icon pointing down next to "iPad V" and a window will pop up. Click "Create Alternate Layout."

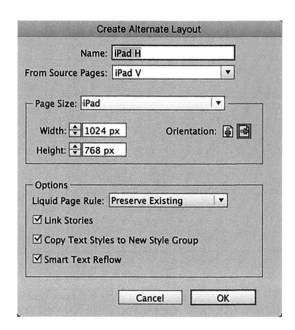

Figure 9.21

Click "OK" in the bottom right.

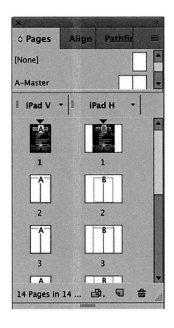

Figure 9.22

In the "Pages" window, you can see that the alternate layout has been created. Now, you can choose to change the layout manually.

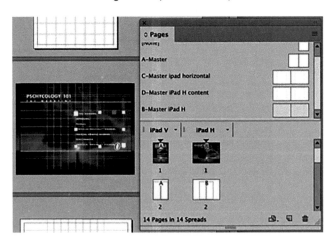

Figure 9.23

You can see in the "Pages" window that page 1 of iPad H has been edited to fit the horizontal cover option. In addition, the location of the text and the grid itself have changed to create an appealing design for the horizontal cover. The vertical and horizontal covers need to complement each other. In this case, I am using the same typeface, size, and background image. The only difference is the arrangement of the type. Overall, they are both very similar and maintain the core of the design structure.

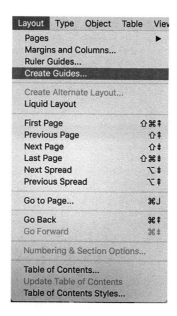

Figure 9.24

If you need to fix the Guides of the Horizontal Layout, go to the top menu, select "Layout," and choose "Create Guides" from the drop-down menu.

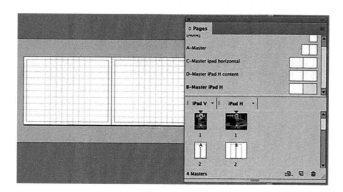

Figure 9.25

Make sure you choose the Master page of the Horizontal iPad, so that you can adjust the Guides of the document.

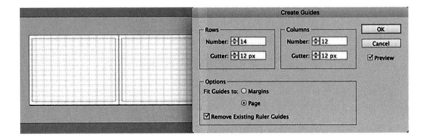

Figure 9.26

Go to the top menu, select "Layout," and choose "Create Guides." If they are already guides, then check the bottom-left box where it says "Remove Existing Ruler Guides." Then, you will be able to see the new rows and columns. Once you set them according to your design structure, click "OK."

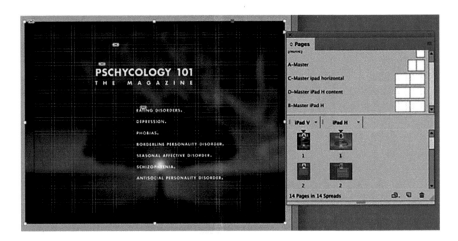

Figure 9.27

The cover of the horizontal layout has been adjusted including the guides of this layout.

Table of Contents or Navigation

The table of contents is an overview of what is inside the magazine, and there are many creative ways to design one. The easiest method is using a software reader such as a Kindle, which already provides a page-scroll navigation so that the reader can easily navigate the magazine. This type of magazine is usually not too interactive but it can have easy access for any reader. This type of magazine is used because the file size and the memory space do not create conflict with the user's device. Sometimes a magazine can be so large that it could crash a phone or tablet. It really depends on the expertise of the designer when adding images and files to the magazine's contents.

Table of Contents

There are many ways of adding pagination, and which one you choose depends on the type of publisher you will be using. Following are two tutorials, the first of which shows you how to create a table of contents in an EPUB and the second of which illustrates how to create a consistent navigation that allows the content to be easily accessed regardless of what page the user is using in an interactive PDF.

Setting Up Pages for the Table of Contents

When setting up the table of contents, have a list of chapters and the location of the chapters ready. The great advantage of using a table of contents is that if you change the chapter pages or rearrange them, then the table will automatically readjust itself according to the changes you have made.

Step 1: Placing the Chapters
Before creating the table of contents, it is necessary to have the title of the chapters and their respective pages (Figure 9.28).

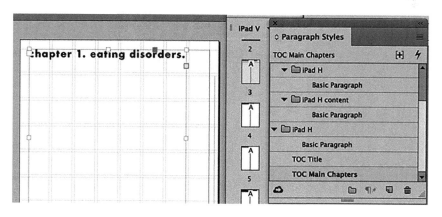

Figure 9.28

At the beginning of this chapter, the text title for Chapter 1 "eating disorders" has been created. Add the rest of the chapters in the pages. In this example, there are a total of seven chapters.

Step 2: Creating Character and Paragraph Styles

Before creating a table of contents, the text must have a style. For short pieces of text such as a title, you can create a character style; for longer pieces of text, you can use a paragraph style. For more detail, see Chapter 7 and look for *Setting Type and Learning to Apply Character and Paragraph Style* (Figures 9.29 and 9.30).

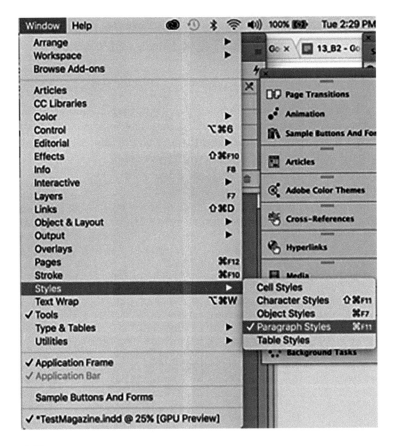

Figure 9.29

Go to the top menu and select "Window." From the drop-down menu, choose "Styles" and then click "Paragraph Styles."

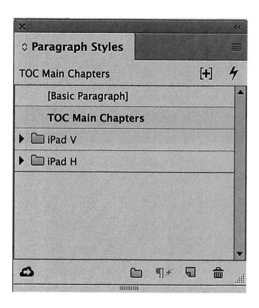

Figure 9.30

When the "Paragraph Styles" window opens, choose the top-right hamburger menu and select "New Paragraph Style." Then, create a new Paragraph Style: In this example, we titled it "TOC Main Chapters." Next, apply this to all the title chapters of the InDesign files. This method can be applied in a similar way when working with Character Styles.

Setting the Table of Contents for an Interactive EPUB, PDF, and SWF

Setting up the table of contents to export an interactive PDF is very simple if you already have Character Styles and/or Paragraph Styles for the table of contents page (Figures 9.31 through 9.34).

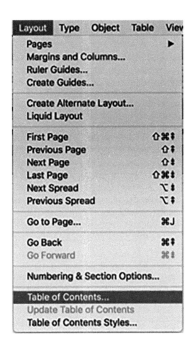

Figure 9.31

From the top menu, select "Layout," and then choose "Table of Contents..."

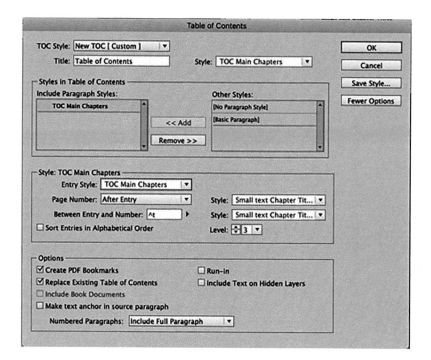

Figure 9.32

The Table of Contents window has four main parts. The section "TOC Style" allows you to use a default New TOC. In this example, you can see that the table of contents at the top is using the New TOC, and right below there is "Title." In the textbox, you can place any text you want; in this case, I typed *Table of Contents*. Next to it, you can set a main Paragraph Style (I am using a Paragraph that I already created: "TOC Main Chapters"). Then, in the Title section "Styles in Table of Contents," you can add more Paragraph Styles but in my case I am using the same "TOC Main Chapters."

The section below is "Style: TOC Main Chapters." In this example, I am using "TOC Main chapters," but feel free to use another Style. Under it, there is a section "Page Number," and next to it there is a "Style" option. In there, you can create a different Style solely for page numbers. Then, below there is a section "Between Entry and Number." You have the option to add a "Style" next to it as well.

The last section gives you "Options," but you probably want to leave it the way it is. Where it says "Numbered Paragraphs," there are a total of three options: Include Full Paragraph, Include Numbers Only, and Exclude Numbers.

Once everything has been set, click "OK" at the top-right side of the window.

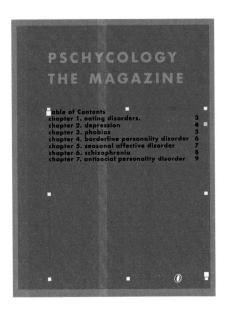

Figure 9.33

Look at the page where the table of contents has been populated with text automatically by InDesign. Now, if you add pages to the chapters, the table of contents will automatically be updated as well.

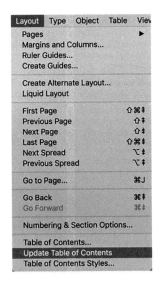

Figure 9.34

If you made changes to the Character or Paragraph Styles, you can easily update the table of contents by going to "Layout" and selecting "Update Table of Contents."

9. Magazines and Books

Exporting Test of the Table of Contents as EPUB

Figures 9.35 through 9.37.

Figure 9.35

From the top menu, select "File" and then click "Export."

Figure 9.36

The "Export" window will pop up and require you to give it a name in the "Save as" textbox. When you have done this, click "Save."

Figure 9.37

Automatically, the EPUB application on your computer will pop up and open the file. If you click the second icon at the top, it will provide you with thumbnails at the bottom with each chapter, and you can easily navigate each chapter using the thumbnails located at the bottom. In addition, you can see the page numbers at the bottom right of each page.

Exporting Test of the Table of Contents as PDF

Figures 9.38 through 9.43.

Figure 9.38

From the top menu, select "File" and then click "Export."

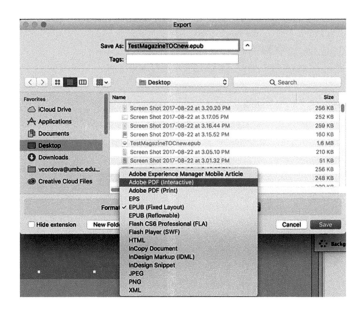

Figure 9.39

In the "Export" window, select "Adobe PDF (Interactive)."

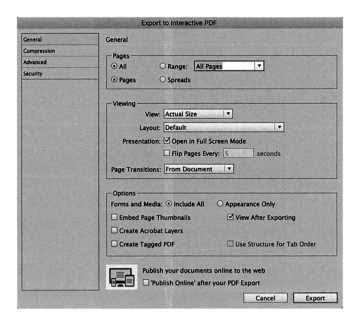

Figure 9.40

The Interactive PDF Export window will pop up. In this case, I am not making any changes, so I simply need to click "Export."

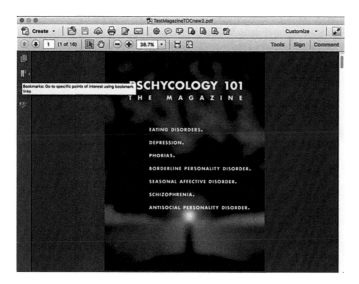

Figure 9.41

The PDF file will automatically open. On the left side of the Acrobat file, you will see a Bookmark icon. In the above-mentioned image, there is a pop-up box on the left highlighting the Bookmark icon. Click on the "Bookmark icon."

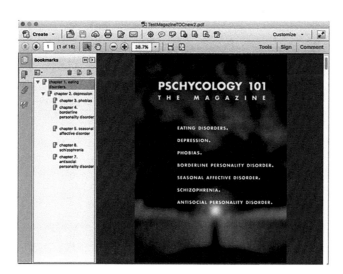

Figure 9.42

The Bookmark window will open on the left side and then you will see the magazine's table of contents. It is very easy to navigate using the bookmarks in the PDF file.

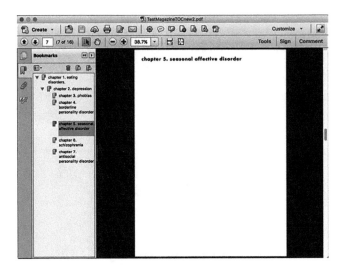

Figure 9.43

I clicked "chapter 5. seasonal affective disorder" and it automatically took me to that chapter in the PDF file.

Exporting Test of the Table of Contents as SWF

Figures 9.44 through 9.48.

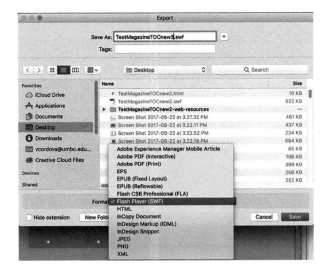

Figure 9.44

After clicking "File" in the top menu, select "Export" and a window will pop up. Select "Flash Player (SWF)."

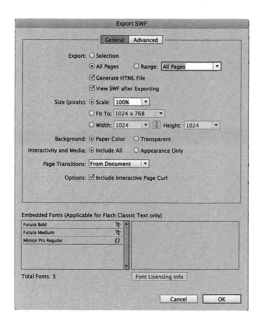

Figure 9.45

A window will pop up. I did not make any changes and simply clicked "OK." If you want to make some changes, feel free to do so. Click "OK" when you have finished.

Figure 9.46

Your default browser will automatically open the SWF file in an HTML page.

Figure 9.47

Using the arrows on your keyboard, you can go to the next page. In the table of contents, each chapter will take you to the respective page.

Figure 9.48

In the above-mentioned image, it shows what happened when I clicked the Chapter 3 hyperlink in the table of contents: It took me to Chapter 3.

9. Magazines and Books

Columns

When designing a magazine, keep in mind whether the user will be reading it vertically or horizontally, or both. In addition, consider what type of file the reader will be using (e.g., EPUB or PDF). It is necessary to create reflowable text when it is published for mobile devices. Keep in mind that the typography needs to be larger than print, so bring more spacing between lines and more kerning between characters as well (Figures 9.49 through 9.53).

When prototyping a magazine, you can restrict the readability design to only vertical or horizontal (sometimes you can provide both and it will vary according to the content and the limitations of the images, text, etc.).

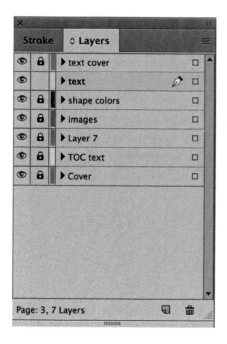

Figure 9.49

Before adding columns of text, it is important to lock the layers to make it easier to work with only text.

Figure 9.50

In the Tool Box of InDesign, click on the "T" icon, which allows you to create boxes in which to place text.

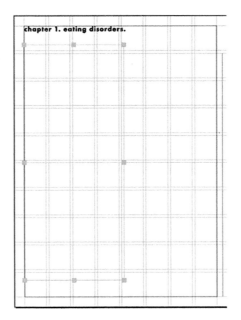

Figure 9.51

Create the textbox for the first column. When creating the textbox, make sure you align it with the grid so the layout and the structure are consistent.

Figure 9.52

In some cases, the textbox may be too small to contain all the text. At the bottom right of the textbox, there is a red plus icon inside a square. When we click on the plus sign a small icon will show up and automatically the cursor has the text not fitting in the textbox. At that moment, you create another textbox and if the plus sign continues to show up at the bottom of the new textbox, then you continue creating textboxes until the plus sign disappears. Once the plus sign no longer shows in the textboxes, no more text is left.

Figure 9.53

Example of two columns on a page.

Anchor Images in the Text

When images are placed in the text, it is necessary to use anchors. When you place an image, make sure there is enough space around and between the text. Images can bring chaos to the pages, but with anchors the text and the images can be reflowable as well (Figures 9.54 and 9.55).

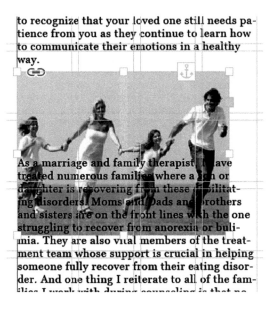

Figure 9.54

An image has been brought in between the text and an anchor icon can be seen in the top-right corner of the image box. When we click on the anchor, it will automatically align with the top of the text and will help create order and legibility in the space.

In addition, there can be whole new levels of social pressure around being thin that you're just not used to dealing with.

Your loved one cannot be in a position to communicate effectively with you until that stabilization and maintenance have occurred. After that stabilization of eating patterns occurs, the real family work can develop. It is important to recognize that your loved one still needs patience from you as they continue to learn how to communicate their emotions in a healthy way.

As a marriage and family therapist, I have treated numerous families where a son or daughter is recovering from these debilitating disorders. Moms and Dads and brothers and sisters are on the front lines with the one struggling to recover from anorexia or bulimia. They are also vital members of the treatment team whose support is crucial in helping someone fully recover from their eating disorder. And one thing I reiterate to all of the families I work with during counseling is that no one is to blame for the disorder but everyone can assist in the recovery.

Most eating disorders are anathema to those who do not have one, but certain food-related illnesses are particularly alarming and baffling to the public at large. PICA is certainly one of them.

This led me to wonder- how hard must mindfulness be for those that look toward these holidays with dread rather than joyous anticipation? While there are many reasons that the holiday season is challenging for people, for the purposes of this article, I will focus on those individuals whose difficulty around the holidays is related to their eating disorders.

We all have well learned that while there is excitement about being with family and friends during the Holiday season, there is also a certain amount of stress. For those who are feeling "pretty good" emotionally, the holidays can enhance those positive emotional and relationship experiences.

The holidays can be a stressful time for anyone, regardless of whether an eating disorder is involved in your life. Commonly, there are plans to be made, family members and loved ones to visit with, parties and social gatherings to attend, gifts to buy, meals to make, and often inundation with food.

Thyroid problems are extremely common population-wide and are an issue for some in recovery from eating disorders as well. However, the type of dysfunction that occurs in the general population and those with a history of an eating disorder are not usually the same.

Today, we are bombarded with photos of today's "beautiful women" in magazines, commercials, TV shows, movies and online photos. These women that represent today's standard of beauty look very different from women of the past. The women displayed on the nationally broadcasted Victoria's Secret runway shows each year epitomize the extreme standards the media portrays as "sexy" and "beautiful."

Figure 9.55

Example of ending an article in a magazine.

Metadata

When you save digital files, it is necessary to add metadata. Metadata helps the file to be found and searched easily in an online store (Figures 9.56 and 9.57).

Figure 9.56

Go to "File" and from the drop-down menu, select "File Info..."

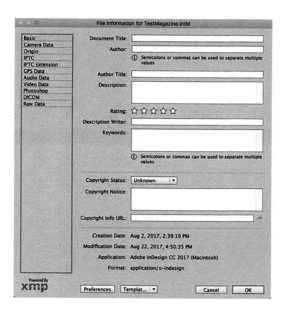

Figure 9.57

A window will pop up with a variety of textboxes to fill out.

Online Magazine

For more information about websites and apps, visit Chapter 11.

Magazine as an App

For more information on mobile apps, visit Chapter 12.

Working with EPUB Files for Magazines

When publishing magazines, some of the most popular places are Apple iBookstore, Barnes & Noble NOOK Book Store, and Google Play eBookstore.

Working with .MOBI Files for Magazines

The .MOBI file works with Amazon Kindle App and supports Windows, Mac, and mobile devices for further information about electronic publishing, visit The International Digital Publishing Forum at http://idpf.org/.

Video

For more information on videos, please visit Chapter 6.

Sound

For more information on sound, please visit Chapter 5.

Animation

For more information on animation, please visit Chapters 10 and 11.

Columns and Hyphenation

When creating Paragraph Styles, you can set the amount of hyphenation allowed in the paragraphs (Figure 9.58).

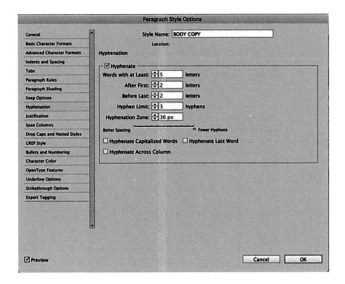

Figure 9.58

When you are creating a paragraph style (for tutorials, visit Chapter 7). On the left menu of the Paragraph Style Options, there is "Hyphenation." In that section you can reduce the hyphenation. If you unclick the Hyphenate checkbox, all the columns using this paragraph will stop using hyphenation.

Articles

Creating articles is very helpful for all types of interactive publications because articles allow us to keep the content the way we want it to be. It is almost like using the function group because when you place images, shapes, or text in an article, they will not be disorganized but rather aligned, as expected. This function is extremely helpful when files are being exported for EPUB, SWF, and HTML files because things can easily move around (Figures 9.59 through 9.68).

Figure 9.59

When text images and shapes overlap, it is necessary to use articles because this is the only way to keep objects the way they were designed.

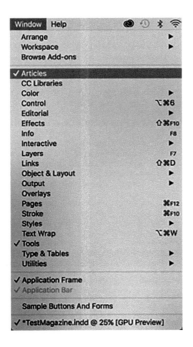

Figure 9.60

From the top menu, click on "Window" and then select "Articles" from the drop-down menu.

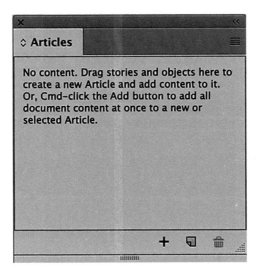

Figure 9.61

The "Articles" window opens and that is where you can add articles.

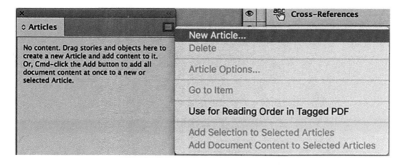

Figure 9.62

Click on the hamburger menu icon located at the top right and select "New Article..."

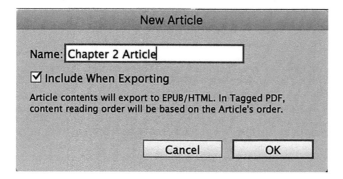

Figure 9.63

A "New Article" window will pop up, and in the "Name" textbox, you can type the name of the article. In this case, the name is "Chapter 2 Article." Once the article has a name, click "OK."

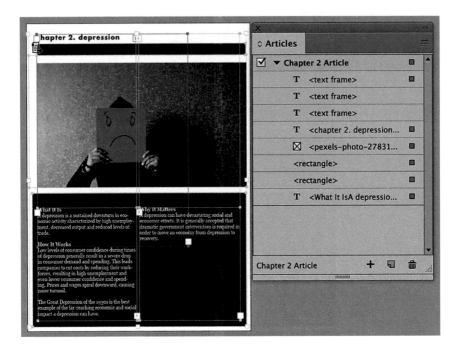

Figure 9.64

In "Document," select the text, images, and shape colors you want to include in the article. When you know what to place in an article, select the objects and drag them to the article. They will be automatically listed like layers in the article, as can be seen in the right-hand window. Usually, you have to click twice on each layer to check and make sure it is in the order you want. For example, if the image is all the way at the bottom in the layers, it will not be correctly placed and will not look as is seen in the document. Be aware that you can have more than one page in one article. You can place several pages and objects in an article as long as they all belong to a specific section.

Figure 9.65

From the top menu, click "File," and then choose "Export" from the drop-down menu.

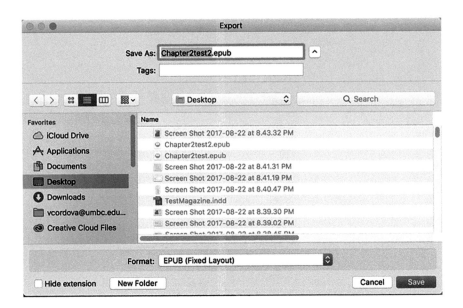

Figure 9.66

The "Export" window will pop up and then you will give the file a name. Select EPUB (Fixed Layout) in the "Format" section and then click "Save."

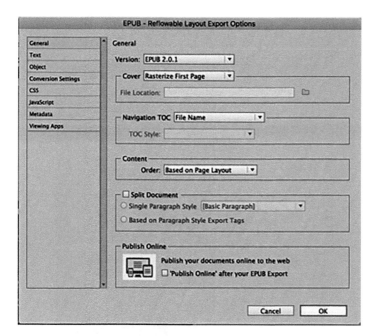

Figure 9.67

The EPUB window will pop up and you can set the EPUB version you need. In this case, I am using EPUB 2.0.1. and the "Navigation TOC" provides a drop-down menu where you can select the TOC you have created for the InDesign file. In addition, the EPUB has an option to publish online, and if you check the "Publish Online" box, it will automatically take you to share the file online. In this case, leave the "Publish Online" box unchecked and click "OK."

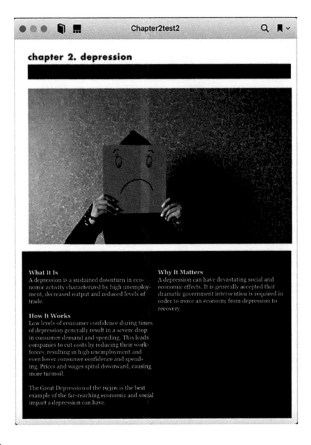

Figure 9.68

The EPUB (Fixed Layout) window shows this chapter the way we want it because the "Article" in InDesign is in use.

Digital Publishing Suite

Digital Publishing Suite was a tool used for digital publishing until 2015, but it is no longer available. If you were looking to learn how to create folios or anything that DPS used to do, please note that it is only available for Business Enterprise. For more information visit: http://www.adobe.com/mt/products/digital-publishing-suite-pro/buying-guide-pricing.html.

Websites and Web Apps

Creating prototypes of websites in InDesign is a very simple process that can take minutes, and the work can be previewed easily as either a small web format (SWF) file or an Interactive PDF. Your client will be able to see easily the necessary functionality of the website or web app using page links, animation, transitions, and object states. When working in InDesign, make sure all measurements are set to pixels.

Please visit Chapter 7 to learn more about layout and creating a grid structure for your pages. You can also find in-depth tutorials in Chapter 7 on setting up pages and master pages, placing images, setting type, and buttons that work with actions. It may be useful to revisit that chapter to go over those tutorials, as they will help you to understand better the tutorials in this chapter.

Setting Up Files

Figures 10.1 through 10.4.

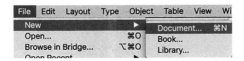

Figure 10.1

To create a new document, go to the top menu and select "File," then click "New," and finally choose "Document."

Figure 10.2

Once in the "New Document," choose "Web" from the drop menu.

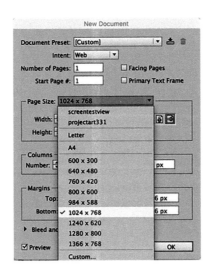

Figure 10.3

In this example, the page size section is going to be set to 1024 × 768. This measurement means that there are 1024 pixels by 768 pixels. Once you have set this measurement, InDesign will automatically use pixels in this document, including when setting the rulers or creating shapes. Even the typography measurement will be in pixels as well.

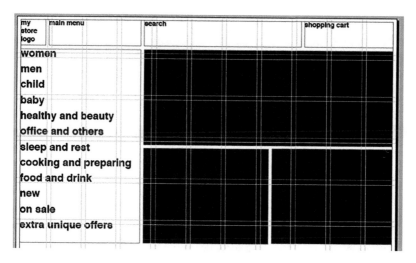

Figure 10.4

Here you can see the desktop layout size of a website prototype.

Extending the Document Size

If you think the vertical or horizontal spaces are too small, it is important to look at the document setup and make changes, as shown in Figures 10.5 through 10.7.

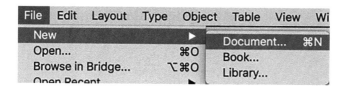

Figure 10.5

From the top menu, select "File" and then "New." In the submenu, choose "Document."

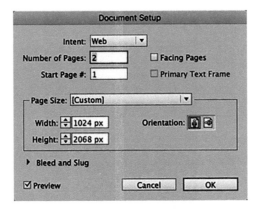

Figure 10.6

The "Document Setup" window will show up, and it is here where you can manage the width and height, resetting these at any time. In this example, I am changing the height to 2068 pixels because the website I am working on has a lot of content and it needs to be readjusted in length: Therefore, the length needs to be changed. When this happens, the grid system needs to be readjusted as well. Therefore, plan in advance and make sketches so you have a better idea of the actual size of the page. Set boundaries and limits so your design can be consistent throughout the website.

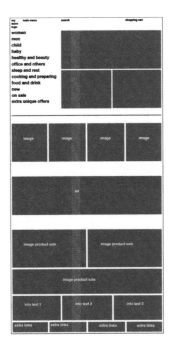

Figure 10.7

Here you can see a new revised layout for a desktop browser.

Mobile Website

The following example shows the view of a mobile website, which is very limited in size and layout (Figure 10.8).

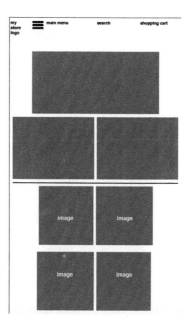

Figure 10.8

The mobile layout needs to have only one column of text. Usually, this is the maximum that a mobile device can fit on its screen while remaining legible, especially if it is a handheld device.

Navigation

Page Links

When creating page links for a website, it is necessary to have several pages that will show the transition from one page to the next or even if a drop menu will be created. Each page needs to show the user incrementally how to interact with the website (Figure 10.9).

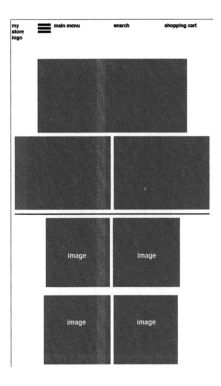

Figure 10.9

The design of the website provides four main links in the top navigation: my store logo, main menu, search, and shopping cart.

Stage One: Main Menu

In the next tutorial, the main menu hamburger icon provides a list of links that will take the user to the main parts of the website. In this tutorial, the hamburger icon provides a drop menu and it also gives you the option to go inside other pages in the submenu (Figures 10.10 through 10.13).

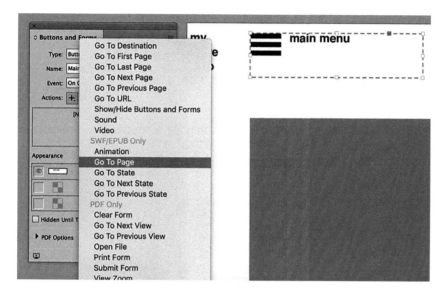

Figure 10.10

Select the main menu icon and go into the window in the top menu. Then, select "Interactive" and choose "Buttons and Forms." As in chapter 7, start by choosing "Button," give it a name, choose "On Click" in the "Event" box, and in the "Actions" section, choose "Go To Page."

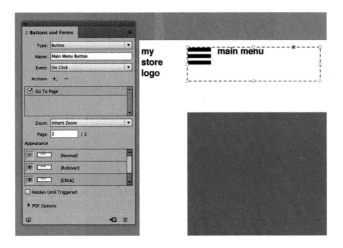

Figure 10.11

Next, type the desired page into the textbox (e.g., 2). In "Appearance," make sure to activate the eye icon, which activates "Normal," "Rollover," and "Click."

Figure 10.12

If you need a reminder of how many pages you have, or if you wish to add or delete pages, then go into the top menu in InDesign and select "Window" and then select "Pages."

Figure 10.13

This is page 2, which opens the hamburger menu and allows the user to see the submenu that provides 12 other categories.

Stage Two: Main Menu Open

Figures 10.14 through 10.19.

Figure 10.14

Now that the hamburger menu is open, we have to create a button that closes as well. This is located in "Page 2." By selecting the "X icon" and making it a button, it will go back to Page 1. The option to choose to give that action to the icon is located in the left window, titled "Buttons and Forms."

Figure 10.15

Once both actions are given, they can be tested by selecting the option at the top right in InDesign, titled "Publish Online."

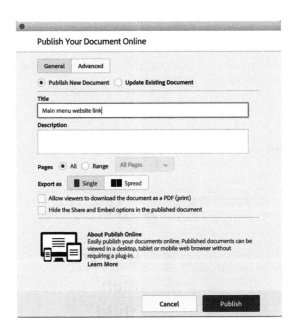

Figure 10.16

A window will pop-up titled "Publish Your Document Online." Select "Publish New Document" and give it a title. In this example, I have called it "Main menu website link," and I have selected "All" in Pages and also decided to export it as "Single" and select "Publish." This is a quick way to preview anytime when you are work-ing, so that you can test your file. It is necessary to test over and over to make sure buttons work and check everything is in order. When the user or client views it, they will observe a smooth transition and get an understanding of what the document is trying to do and communicate.

Figure 10.17

In the "Publish Online" window, you can see that the document has been uploaded online. Now, you can share the link with others by selecting "Copy" and then pasting it anywhere. You can also share through social media or even email. By selecting "View Document," a browser will open and show the document.

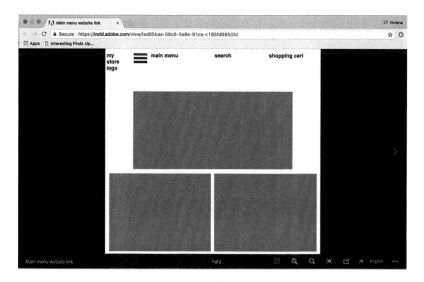

Figure 10.18

When the document has opened in the browser, click the hamburger menu.

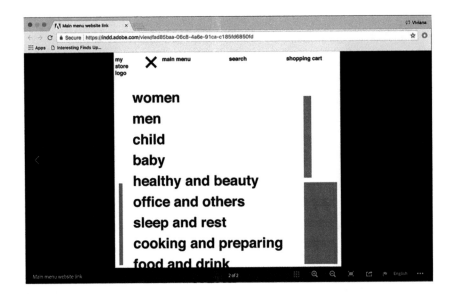

Figure 10.19

The window will go to page 2, which shows the main menu with the 12 categories.

10. Websites and Web Apps

Creating a Home Page Button

Figure 10.20.

Figure 10.20

Select "my store logo," which is the main mark for the company website. This should always direct the user to the main home page, regardless of where the user is. In the above-mentioned image, you can see the steps to be chosen in the "Buttons and Forms" window. Note that the button will always go to "page 1."

Creating Buttons to Navigate to Other Pages from a Submenu

When creating buttons for submenus or secondary navigation, it is important to make sure that each button is easy to click and to interact with. Size, location, and contrast (behind, front, and to the sides) are very important.

Part I: Creating a Button for the Submenu

Figures 10.21 through 10.27.

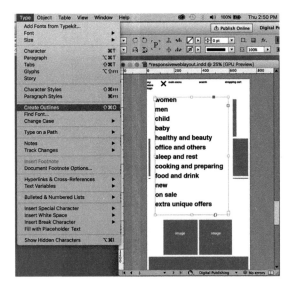

Figure 10.21

In this example, you can see a textbox that has 12 lines of text. If you select this to become a button, then the whole textbox will be only one button. Therefore, it is very important to break the text so that you are able to select each line individually by creating 12 buttons that will take the user to 12 different pages. Go to the main menu and select "Type," and from the submenu select "Create Outlines." This option will convert the letterforms to single shapes.

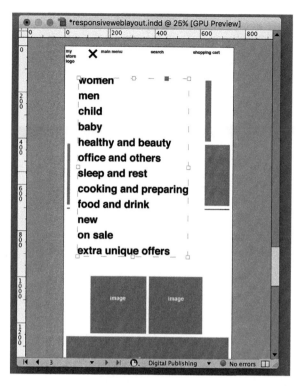

Figure 10.22

After the letterforms become outlines, all 12 lines of text are still grouped.

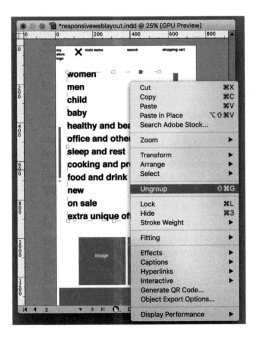

Figure 10.23

Select the textbox and press control+click in it. A menu will appear, and from there you should select "Ungroup." This option will automatically give you the freedom to move the letterforms or regroup them in any way you want.

Figure 10.24

Here, you can see that all letterforms are ungrouped.

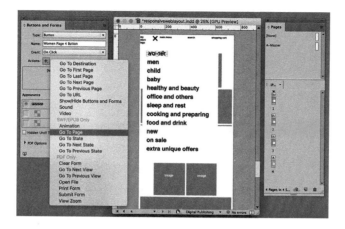

Figure 10.25

Select the first group of shapes ("women") and open the "Buttons and Forms" window. This will allow "women" to become a button and it will go to page 3. On the right side, you can see that the "Pages" window is also open, and more pages can be created and/or organized as more buttons are created to make it easy to navigate between the pages.

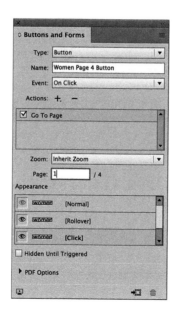

Figure 10.26

In the "Buttons and Forms" window, the "women" button has been created by looking at the setting. The only change that needs to be made is that in the "Page" section, we need to type "3" so that the button goes to page 3, which is the "women" section.

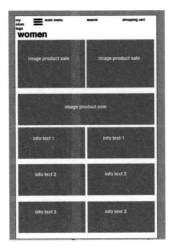

Figure 10.27

Here we can see the "women" page.

What Can You Do with Interactive Options?

Using buttons and object states together creates so much flexibility and it also allows you to create a wide range of buttons and other ways to show interactivity on a website or web app. The following example shows how object states and buttons work together and also demonstrates how other functions can be used, such as scrollbars and page transitions. Once you go through all these tutorials, it will be very easy to create interactivity and functionality in your prototype, and when you test it with users, it will be easy for them to understand the purpose of the prototype. The most important part of this stage is for you to create sketches and brainstorm ahead of time. When you have finished sketching and organizing the steps that the user must go through to interact with the web app or website, it will be very easy to make it happen with the interactive tools in InDesign.

Introduction to Object States

Object states allow you to have interactions within the page beyond those that buttons enable. For example, if you want to have a gallery of images without creating more pages, you can achieve this by using this function. Following are the instructions that will guide you to create a gallery or slideshow using object states and buttons that allow you to control the states where the images will be nested (Figure 10.28).

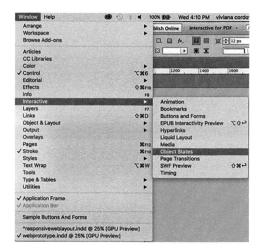

Figure 10.28

Go to "Window" in the top menu and select "Interactive," and then from its drop menu select "Object States." A window will pop up in the front.

Creating a Shoe Gallery

Figure 10.29.

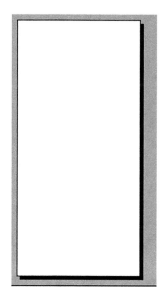

Figure 10.29

Create a new web document in InDesign. The document's measurements need to be in pixels.

Part I: Creating Object States Using Images

Figures 10.30 through 10.42.

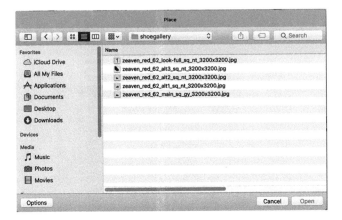

Figure 10.30

In the new document, go to the main menu "File" and select from the crop menu "Place." A window will pop up showing you a directory of your files. You should choose the images that you want to bring by selecting them and clicking open. In this example, five images are being brought to the document.

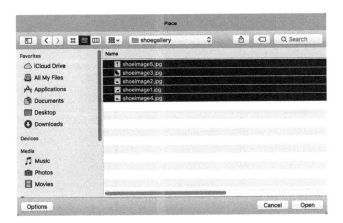

Figure 10.31

Once you have chosen the images from the window, click "Open."

Figure 10.32

Your images will be inserted into the InDesign document. Using the cursor to create a rectangle, the images will be inserted every time a rectangle is created. In this case, by creating five rectangles all images are inserted.

Figure 10.33

Here, you can see that the images are not aligned completely.

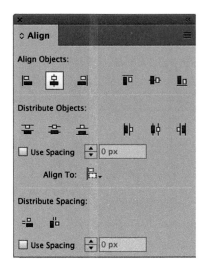

Figure 10.34

In order to align the images, go to "Window" in the top menu and select "Object and Layout," then choose "Align" from the drop menu. All these options help align anything in the document. In this case, all images have to be aligned on top of each other to be able to be seen one after another when the user clicks each button, which will reveal each image.

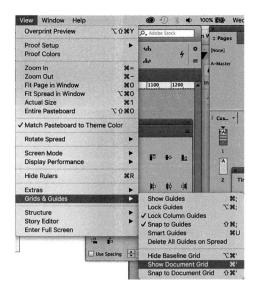

Figure 10.35

In the top menu, select "View." Then, from the drop menu select "Grids & Guides," and choose "Show Document Grid" in the box that appears. This grid is very effective and helps to make sure everything is aligned quickly.

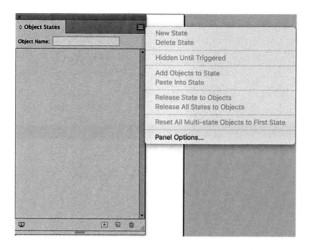

Figure 10.36

From the main menu select "Window," in the submenu select "Interactive," and under it select "Object States." This window provides a menu on the right side after clicking the hamburger menu. The options in this menu are: New State, Delete State, Hidden Until Triggered, Add Objects to State, Paste into State, Release State to Objects, Release All States to Objects, Reset All Multi-State Objects to First State, and Panel Options.

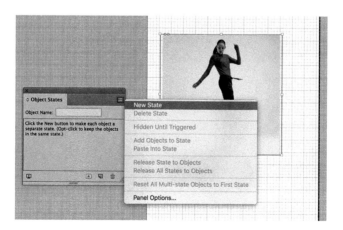

Figure 10.37

After selecting all five images that were aligned one behind the other earlier, now go to the hamburger menu in the "Object States" window and select "New State."

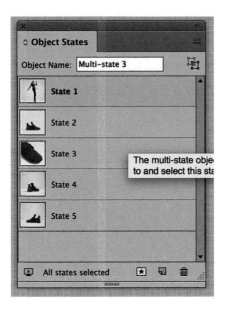

Figure 10.38

The "Object States" window created five states. Here you can see that each image became one state and every single one has a number to distinguish it from the others.

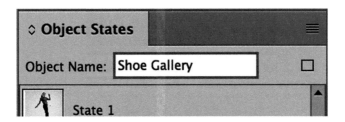

Figure 10.39

Every object state needs a name. As an example, here we use "Shoe Gallery."

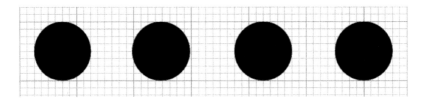

Figure 10.40

Circles are being created and later they will become buttons to activate the object states.

Figure 10.41

The final layout is arranged as follows: The images at the top and the black circles are going to become buttons.

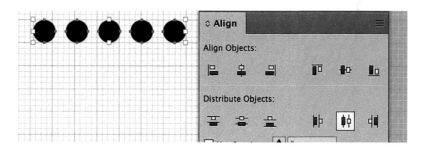

Figure 10.42

All five black circles need to have an equal distance between each other, and using the "Align" window this can be executed through the option "Distribute Horizontal Centers."

Part II: Creating Buttons That Activate Object States

Figures 10.43 through 10.50.

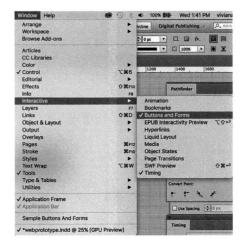

Figure 10.43

Select "Window," then "Interactive," and in the box that appears choose "Buttons and Forms."

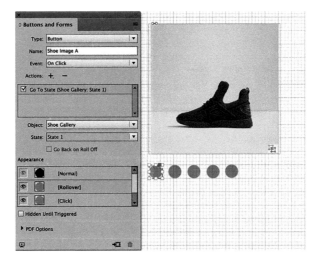

Figure 10.44

The "Buttons and Forms" options will allow you to create buttons. In this example, each circle will be one button. The first button, located on the left is being named "Show Image A" and the "Event" is "On Click." The object chosen is "Shoe Gallery," which is the name of the object state. "State 1" has been selected in "State," and in "Appearance," the eyes of "Normal," "Rollover," and "Click" are being activated.

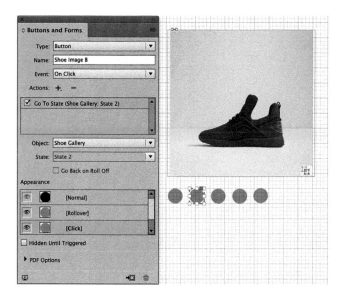

Figure 10.45

Here we see the same process for the second circle from the right. In this case, it is named "Show Image B." In "Actions," select "Go to State (Shoe Gallery: State 2)" from the drop menu. Also, under "Appearance" the eye icon has to be activated for "Normal," "Rollover," and "Click."

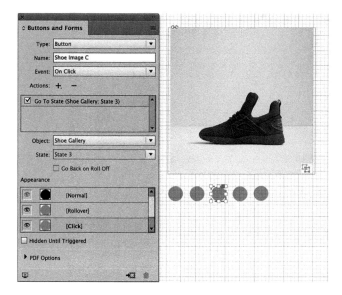

Figure 10.46

Here we see a similar process but the third button has a different name and it goes to a different state, as seen earlier.

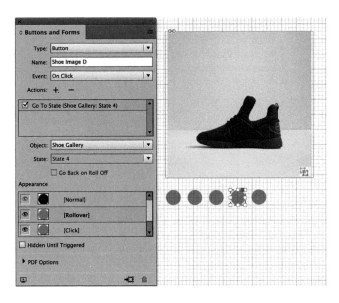

Figure 10.47

Here we see a similar process but the fourth button has a different name and it goes to a different state, as seen previously.

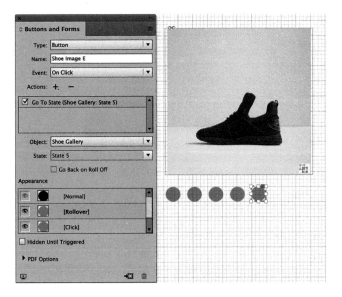

Figure 10.48

Here we see a similar process but the fifth button has a different name and it goes to a different state, as seen earlier.

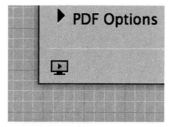

Figure 10.49

In the bottom-left corner of the "Buttons and Forms" window, there is an icon that looks like a TV screen with a play icon inside. This icon allows you to preview the object states in action.

Figure 10.50

Each button, when clicked, will show you each state, from State 1 to State 5.

Creating a Banner AD GALLERY (Object States with Arrows)

Banners in websites and web apps are heavily used, whether for ads or displaying information related to the website or app itself. Regardless of the purpose, users interact with them on a daily basis (Figures 10.51 through 10.59).

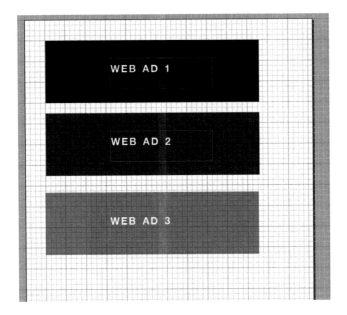

Figure 10.51

All three web ads have to be the same size, width, and height.

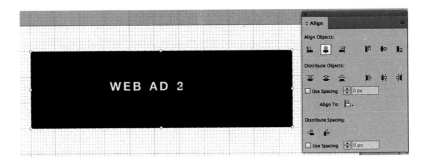

Figure 10.52

Align all ads in the same position on top of each other. Using the "Align" window, select all ads at the same time and click on the icon "Align Horizontal Centers." This will align all the ads.

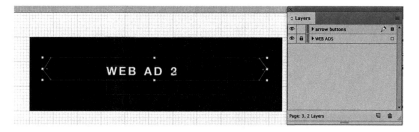

Figure 10.53

We need to create two layers, and we can do this by going to the "Layers" window. The first layer, "WEB ADS," is where the ads will be placed, and the other layer is "arrow buttons." It is important to keep the shapes separate from each other so that there is no confusion when creating buttons.

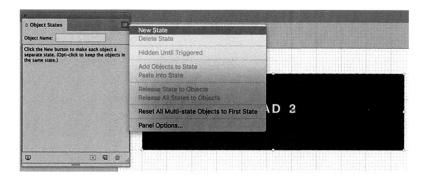

Figure 10.54

After aligning all three ads on top of each other, the "Object States" window will open. You need to select all three ads to create new states. Select "New State" from the hamburger menu.

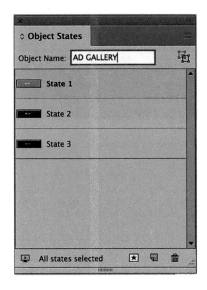

Figure 10.55

It is important to put a name in the "Object Name" box. In this case, it is called "AD GALLERY," and you can see that there are three states.

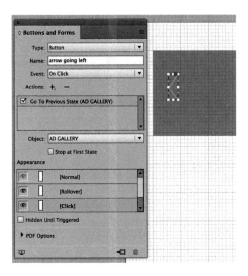

Figure 10.56

Activate the layer "arrow buttons." This will allow you to see the arrow shapes on the page. Here, you can see that the arrow shape pointing left has been selected and is becoming a button. In the "Buttons and Forms" window, the shape is being given a name: "arrow going left." "On Click" has been selected in the "Event" box, in "Actions" the option "Go To Previous State (AD GALLERY)" has been selected, and in "Appearance" all the eye icons have been activated.

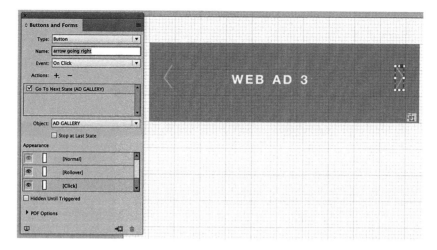

Figure 10.57

You should repeat the same process for the arrow pointing right, although obviously it will require a different name: "arrow going right." Also, in "Actions" you should select "Go To Next State (AD GALLERY)."

Figure 10.58

In the bottom-left corner of the "Buttons and Forms" window there is an icon that looks like a TV screen with a play icon inside. This icon allows you to preview the object states in action. Click this icon.

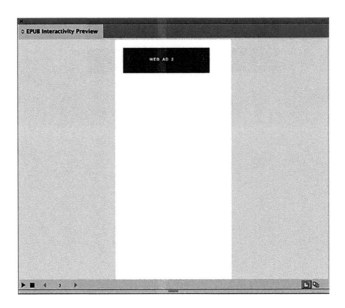

Figure 10.59

Use the preview window to open the file so that you can test whether the arrows actually go to the left and right when the user clicks them.

Animations

Animations are used to bring attention to something. When creating websites or web apps, it is best to avoid blinking animations as they can become a nuisance to the user, and they can be distracting and even encourage the user to close the web app or go to another website.

Animations can be very helpful when you want to alert the user to new information or to something deemed important. For example, when a website has a new look, you should let the user know, and animation is one way of doing this.

Animation can also be useful to get users excited about sales, discounts, or information.

Creating an Alert in a Newspaper Website

Figures 10.60 through 10.74.

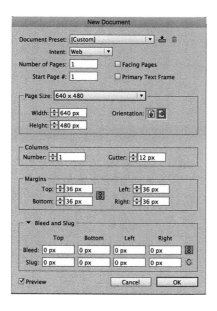

Figure 10.60

From the top menu, select "File" and then "New Document." Follow the options as shown in the figure.

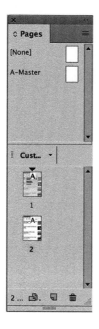

Figure 10.61

Two pages are being created for this prototype.

Figure 10.62

This first page is going to show an ad at the beginning of the website's loading process.

Figure 10.63

The "X" icon will allow the window to be closed and take the user to page 2. In this case, the icon needs to become a button.

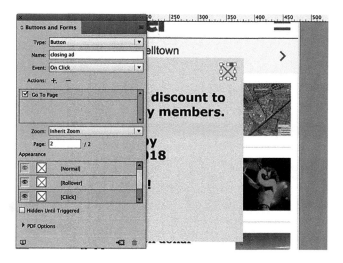

Figure 10.64

After the icon has become a button, call it "closing ad." Then, choose "On Click" in the "Event" box, and in the "Actions" option select "Go To Page." In "Page," select "2," and in "Appearance" you need to activate all the eyes.

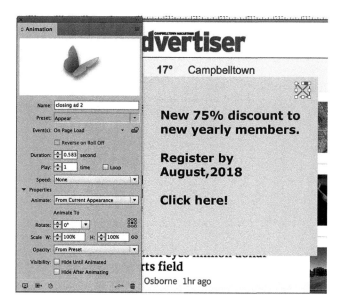

Figure 10.65

In the top menu, select "Window," and then choose the option "Interactive." From the submenu that appears, select "Animation." Select the "X" icon and in the "Preset" box choose "Appear." Next, set the duration to "0.583" s. In the "Properties" section, go to "Animate" and choose "From Current Appearance."

Figure 10.66

Here, we can see that the square with the information in the middle of the website is selected and is also being animated. The animation is called "Yellow Ad" and "Shrink" animation has been selected for the preset. In the "Properties" section, set the "Animate" box as "To Current Appearance," and choose 25% for the scale width and 25% for the height.

Figure 10.67

In the preview, when the user closes the "X" icon the gray square will shrink until it disappears.

Figure 10.68

Select "Publish Online" from the right-hand side of the top menu.

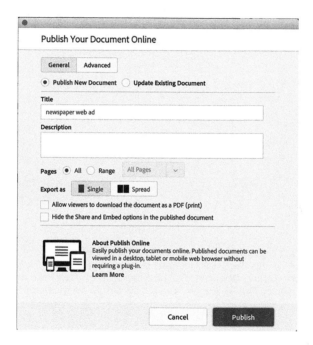

Figure 10.69

A window will pop up and the new publish document is titled "newspaper web ad." In the "Pages" option, select "All" and export as "Single," and then click "Publish."

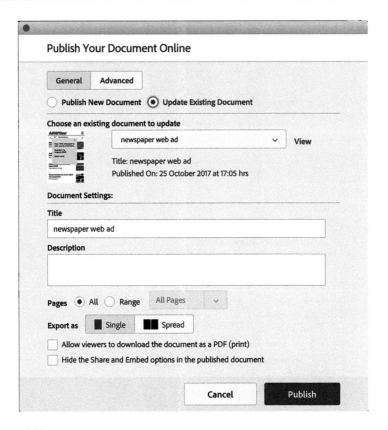

Figure 10.70

If you are already previewing the document and you want to make changes and preview it again, then this is ok. Instead of selecting "Publish New Document," choose "Update Existing Document." Once the file is chosen from the drop menu in the window, select "All" in "Pages," export as "Single," and select "Publish."

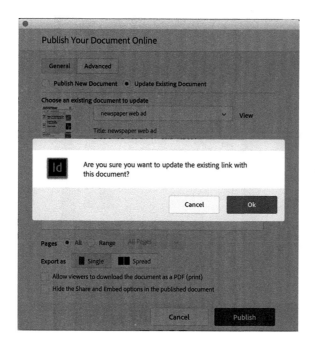

Figure 10.71

A window will pop up asking if you are sure you want to update the document. Click "Ok."

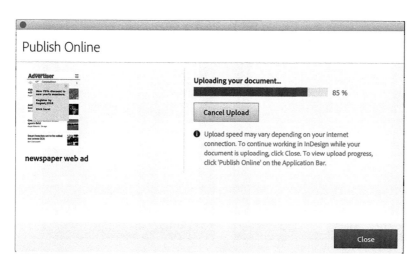

Figure 10.72

The document will be reuploaded again.

Figure 10.73

A window browser will open and the changes will be seen in this version.

Figure 10.74

The ad will initially be visible on page 1, but when the user clicks the "X" icon the ad will shrink and they will be taken to page 2.

Mobile, Desktop, and Custom Apps

Prototypes for all kinds of apps native to the operating system of the device can be rapidly created in simple steps. The layout and graphics need to be effective so the user can understand the visual interaction in the app. No matter the size or purpose of the app, what matters is that all prototypes are clear and concise to communicate the function or message. The wide variety of examples in this chapter including case studies will guide you on how to organize pages and how the buttons can be effectively created.

The options are infinite, and it is not about making a flashy app where things fly around and objects become overly distracting and lacking purpose. Every choice should have an effective reason, and adopting the principle of *simplicity* can help the understanding of the prototype.

This chapter consists of several examples from a rating star app to an ATM app. All the examples in this chapter will help you create prototypes in an easy way and to understand design principles and guide you to make the right choices when creating pages and transitions.

Setting Up Your Document

When setting up a document, it is necessary to set the document in pixels and have a well thought-out structure before starting to work in InDesign. Sketches are important before starting the digital process (Figures 11.1 through 11.7).

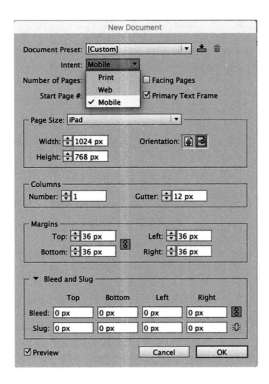

Figure 11.1

Select "File" and "New Document" from the submenu.

11. Mobile, Desktop, and Custom Apps

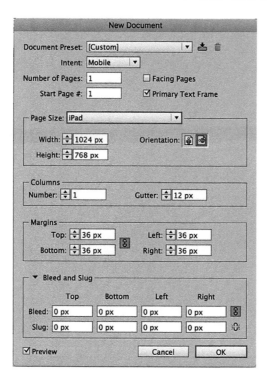

Figure 11.2

In the settings of the "New Document" window, select from the Intent options "Mobile" and in Page Size select—for this example—"iPad." Make sure you check the box "Preview" because this allows you to see a preview of the document you are creating. Once all the decisions have been made, click "OK."

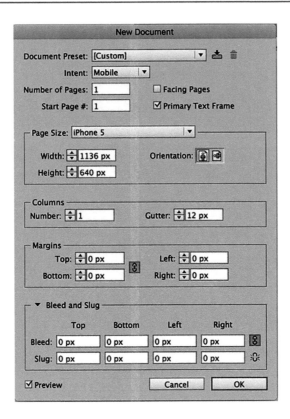

Figure 11.3

In this example, the Intent is "Mobile" and Page Size is "iPhone 5." The Margins option should be 0 pixels on all sides.

Figure 11.4

If you made a mistake and want to change the size of the document, you can always return to "File" from the top menu in InDesign and select "Document Setup."

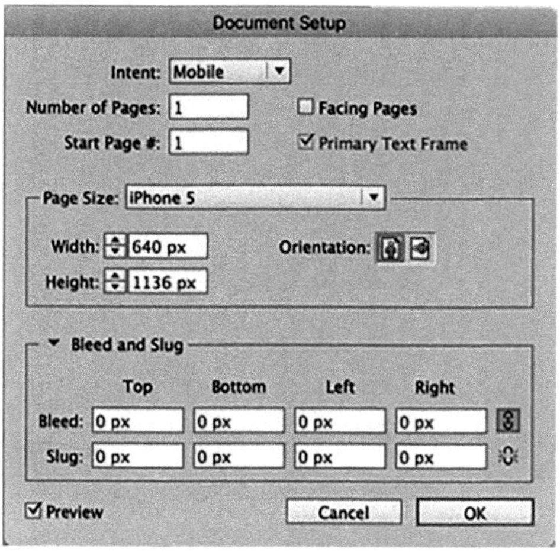

Figure 11.5

"Document Setup" window, where changes can be made.

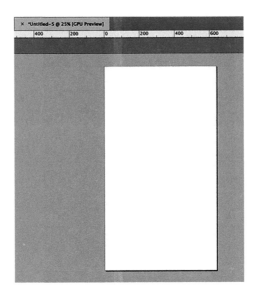

Figure 11.6

The New Document has been created.

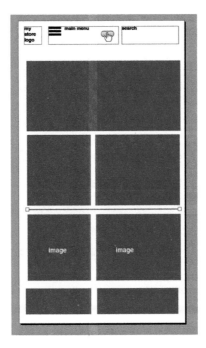

Figure 11.7

A new app wireframe has been created on the first page.

Review App Example

There are several ways in which to review all types of things, and it is necessary to know how to create a review. This example will not only teach you how to carry out a review but also give you ideas of how to apply this method to other types of functions (Figures 11.8 through 11.32).

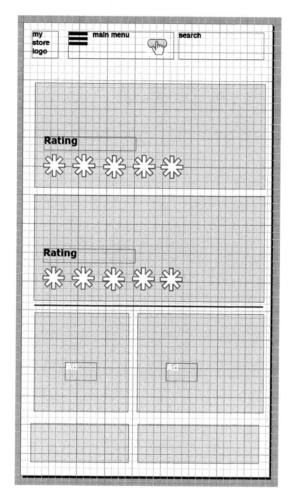

Figure 11.8

The wireframe shows an app prototype that gives ratings.

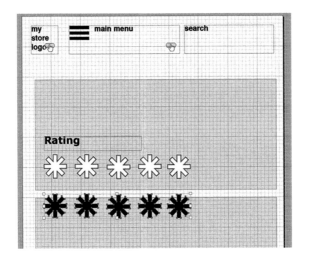

Figure 11.9

In the document, create five black and five white rating stars. The white ones will let the user know that it has not yet been rated, whereas a black star is activated once the user clicks on the review.

Figure 11.10

From the top menu, select "Window" and from the drop-down menu, select "Pages." Create five more copies of the first page.

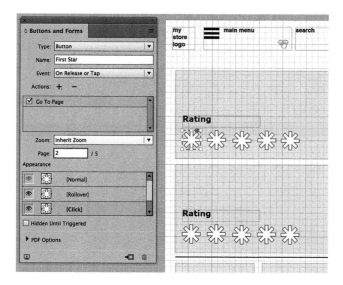

Figure 11.11

Each white star will become a button. In the previous example, the button is called "First Star." In Actions, select "Go to Page" and type in Page "2." Appearance has to activate the eye icons for Normal, Rollover, and Click.

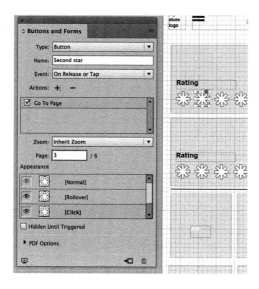

Figure 11.12

The second white star is also a button called "Second Star." In Actions, select "Go To Page" and in Page type "3." Activate the eye icons for Normal, Rollover, and Click in the Appearance section.

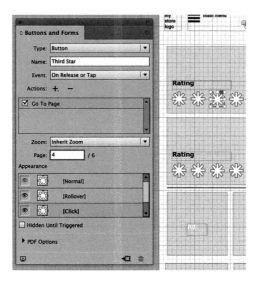

Figure 11.13

The third white star is also a button called "Third Star." In Actions, select "Go To Page" and in Page type "4." Activate the eye icons for Normal, Rollover, and Click in the Appearance section.

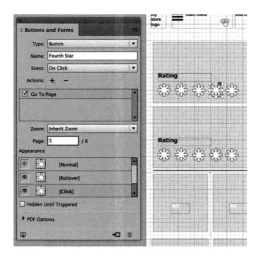

Figure 11.14

The fourth white star is also a button called "Fourth Star." In Actions, select "Go To Page" and in Page type "5." Activate the eye icons for Normal, Rollover, and Click in the Appearance section.

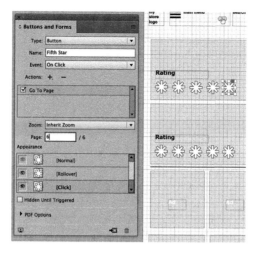

Figure 11.15

The fifth white star is also a button called "Fifth Star." In Actions, select "Go To Page" and in Page type "6." Activate the eye icons for Normal, Rollover, and Click in the Appearance section.

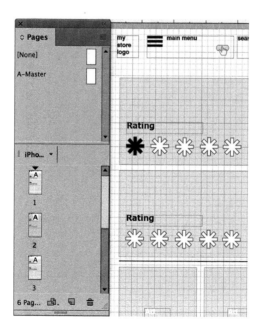

Figure 11.16

In the "Pages" window, select Page 2. Click twice on Page 2 to take you to the InDesign Document on Page 2. On this page, add a black star on top of the white star.

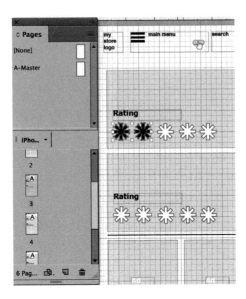

Figure 11.17

In the "Pages" window, select Page 3. Click twice on Page 3 to take you to the InDesign Document on Page 3. On this page, add two black stars on top of the first two first white stars from the left. *Follow the same steps for Page 4.*

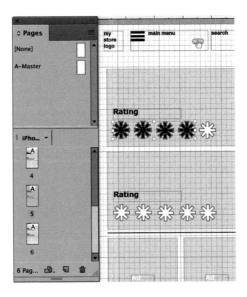

Figure 11.18

In the "Pages" window, select Page 5. Click twice on Page 5 to take you to the InDesign Document on Page 5. On this page, add four black stars on top of the first four first white stars from the left.

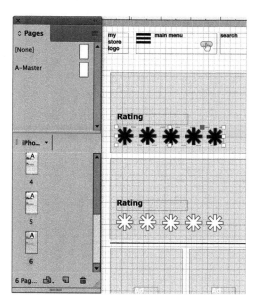

Figure 11.19

In the "Pages" window, select Page 6. Click twice on Page 6 to take you to the InDesign Document on Page 6. On this page, add five black stars on top of the five white stars starting from the left.

Figure 11.20

From the top menu, select "Publish Online."

Figure 11.21

A window will pop up titled "Publish Your Document Online." Give it a title, in this case "Review App." In Pages, select "All." Then, choose Publish to upload the file.

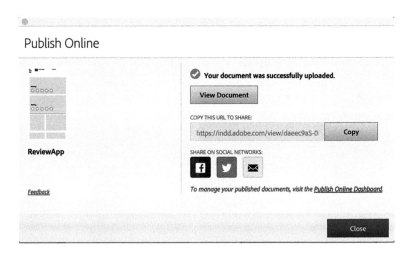

Figure 11.22

After clicking "Publish," another window will open titled "Publish Online." Select "View Document."

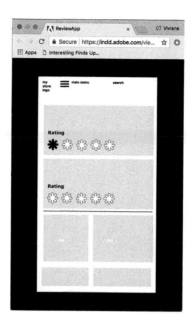

Figure 11.23

The next window shows the wireframe of the prototype. Clicking on the first white star from the left will activate it (i.e., turn it into a black star).

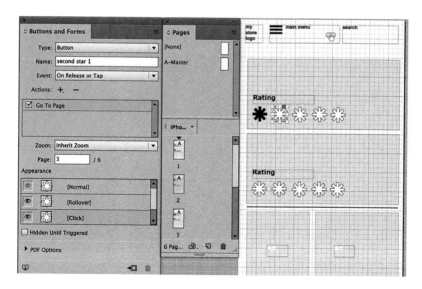

Figure 11.24

The second white star becomes a button titled "second star 1" leading to Page 3. Apply the same method to the other white stars by turning them into buttons.

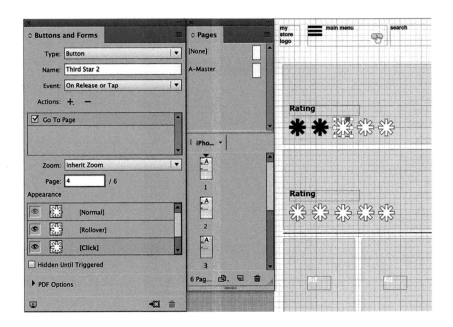

Figure 11.25

The third white star becomes a button titled "third star 1" leading to Page 4.

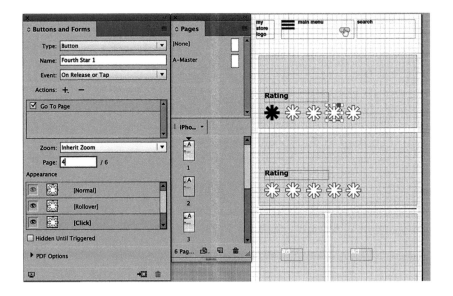

Figure 11.26

The fourth white star becomes a button titled "third star 1" leading to Page 5.

11. Mobile, Desktop, and Custom Apps

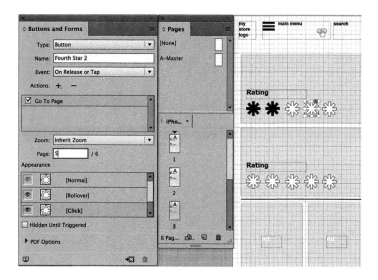

Figure 11.27

The fourth white star becomes a button titled "fourth star 2" leading to Page 5.

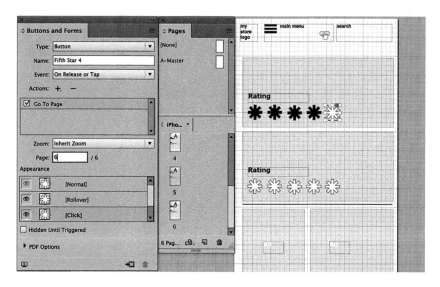

Figure 11.28

The fifth white star becomes a button titled "third star 1" leading to Page 6.

Figure 11.29

To preview the star review, select "Publish Online" from the top menu.

Figure 11.30

The "Publish Your Document Online" window will pop up. Select "Update Existing Document" and the Title Review App. On the pages, select All and Export as "Single." Select "Publish."

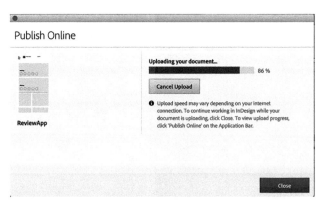

Figure 11.31

The document is uploading during this window.

Figure 11.32

A window browser will open and the stars can be tested. The user can click on each white star and this will activate the black stars.

Creating an Interactive Map App

When creating a nonlinear interactive navigation, the buttons can be created flexibly and the location of the information can be more expressive in the layout. In this example, the world map provides data when each continent is clicked on. This example can inspire various ways in which to create a nonlinear interactive prototype (Figures 11.33 through 11.43).

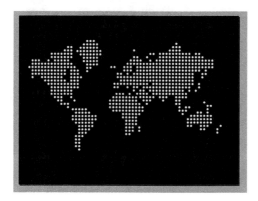

Figure 11.33

World map illustration using the vectors in InDesign.

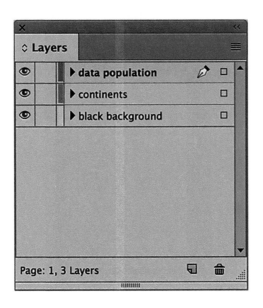

Figure 11.34

In the "Layers" window, create three layers: data population, continents, and black background.

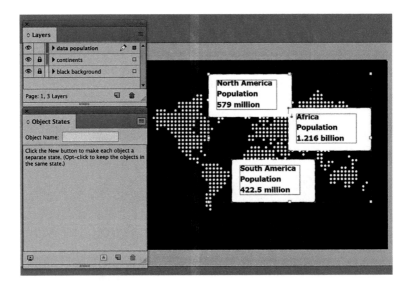

Figure 11.35

In the data population layer, there are three items. Each item needs to become an object state.

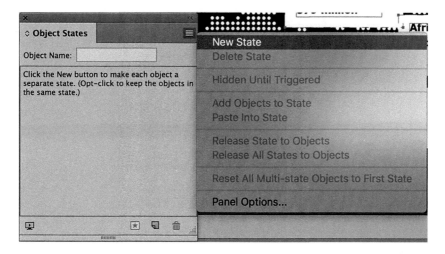

Figure 11.36

Select all three items and from the "Object States" window, click on the hamburger menu and select "New State."

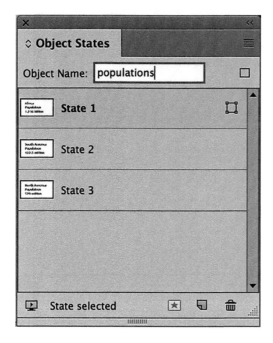

Figure 11.37

The Object will be named "populations" and each State will have its continent information.

Figure 11.38

Opening the "Buttons and Forms" window will allow the North America shape to convert it into a button.

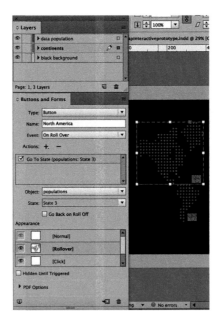

Figure 11.39

The Button is called "North America" and the Event is "On Roll Over." In Actions, select "Go To State (populations: State 3)." In the Object drop-down menu, select "populations" and in State select "3." In addition, in the appearance section, turn on all the eye icons of Normal, Rollover, and Click. In the Rollover layer, the shape of North America can be changed to any color. It has been changed to red in the example. When the user rolls over North America, it will turn red.

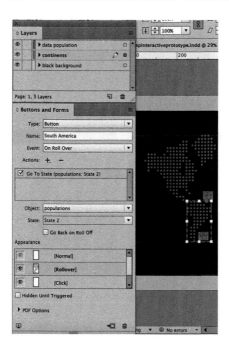

Figure 11.40

The Button is called "South America" and the Event is "On Roll Over." In Actions, select "Go To State (populations: State 2)." In the Object drop-down menu, select "populations" and in State select "2." In addition, in the appearance section, turn on all the eye icons of Normal, Rollover, and Click. In the Rollover layer, the shape of South America can be changed to any color. It has been changed to red in the example. When the user rolls over South America, it will turn red.

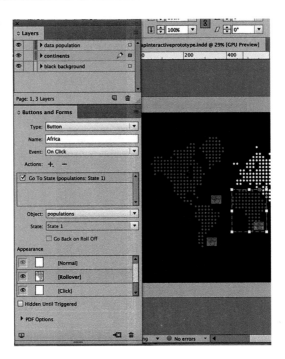

Figure 11.41

The Button is called "Africa" and the Event is "On Roll Over." In Actions, select "Go To State (populations: State 1)." In the Object drop-down menu, select "populations" and in State select "1." In addition, in the appearance section, turn on all the eye icons of Normal, Rollover, and Click. In the Rollover layer, the shape of Africa can be changed to any color. It has been changed to red in the example. When the user rolls over Africa, it will turn red.

Figure 11.42

At the bottom left of the "Buttons and Forms" window is an icon that looks like a TV screen with a play icon inside. This icon allows you to preview the object states in action.

Figure 11.43

"Preview" window showing the object state at work in all three continents.

Case Study Mobile App

The Jot App is an app designed by Hannah Korangkool. This app is a note app that allows you to take notes using various types of background grids including taking handwritten notes on your phone. This app, which has been designed for Android, has a simple color palette of gray tones and red velvet (Figures 11.44 through 11.52).

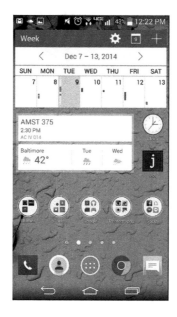

Figure 11.44

Screenshot of a home phone screen and icon size for the phone. The Jot icon has become a button that enters the app. (Courtesy of Hannah Korangkool.)

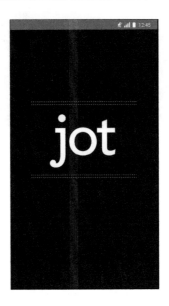

Figure 11.45

Transition page going from the icon to the main app. (Courtesy of Hannah Korangkool.)

Figure 11.46

This page provides three categories: Favorites, Notes, and Stacks. You click a specific icon to choose what kind of note to write. (Courtesy of Hannah Korangkool.)

11. Mobile, Desktop, and Custom Apps

Figure 11.47

This layout provides the keyboards and teaches the user which icon to click to start a checklist. (Courtesy of Hannah Korangkool.)

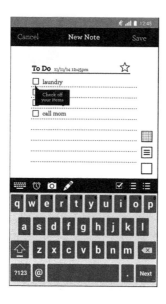

Figure 11.48

This layout guides the user where to check off items in a checklist. (Courtesy of Hannah Korangkool.)

Figure 11.49

This layout shows how to add notes to the favorites section. (Courtesy of Hannah Korangkool.)

Figure 11.50

Reminding the user how to save. (Courtesy of Hannah Korangkool.)

Figure 11.51

Allowing the user to choose from different paper styles. (Courtesy of Hannah Korangkool.)

Figure 11.52

The app also provides a section to doodle. (Courtesy of Hannah Korangkool.)

Case Study Desktop App

Definitely! is an app designed by Mai Huong. This app is located in the top bar as the desktop application is small. It provides translation and other options.

Definitely! Dictionary App

Figures 11.53 through 11.59.

Figure 11.53

Desktop screen showing the icon "d" of Definitely! located at the top of the menu. (Courtesy of Claudia Yee and Mai Huong Huynh-Teage Dictionary! App.)

Figure 11.54

Click the app icon to open a window. Here, the user can interact with the app by searching for a word or choosing other options from the main menu. (Courtesy of Claudia Yee and Mai Huong Huynh-Teage Dictionary! App.)

Figure 11.55

The translator option of the app provides a wide range of options to translate to English and other languages. This example is from English to Vietnamese. (Courtesy of Claudia Yee and Mai Huong Huynh-Teage Dictionary! App.)

Figure 11.56

The translation option of languages is long. (Courtesy of Claudia Yee and Mai Huong Huynh-Teage Dictionary! App.)

Figure 11.57

This screenshot shows the two translation languages. (Courtesy of Claudia Yee and Mai Huong Huynh-Teage Dictionary! App.)

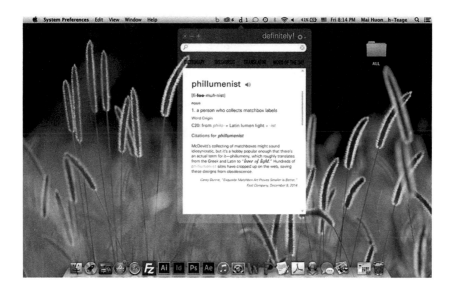

Figure 11.58

Example of a word from the dictionary using a beautiful typographic hierarchy. (Courtesy of Claudia Yee and Mai Huong Huynh-Teage Dictionary! App.)

Figure 11.59

The translate textbox also provides symbols and accents. (Courtesy of Claudia Yee and Mai Huong Huynh-Teage Dictionary! App.)

Case Study ATM App (Custom Size)

Designing an ATM app can be challenging because of the security; moreover, the steps to access an account should be clear. This example designed by Joanna Ashley Espiritu provides a wide range of options. The name of the ATM app is titled "Hello!" and it uses a custom size for the screen. It is a touchscreen and the icons, typography, and layout create a safe easy flow for the user.

Hello! App

Figures 11.60 through 11.82.

Figure 11.60

The introduction page provides four languages to choose from. (Courtesy of Joanna Espiritu and Ciera Earl.)

Figure 11.61

The insert card icon has also an animation that reminds the user to insert the card in the ATM. (Courtesy of Joanna Espiritu and Ciera Earl.)

Figure 11.62

Loading transition page from one page to the next. (Courtesy of Joanna Espiritu and Ciera Earl.)

Figure 11.63

Enter your PIN. This layout also provides the option to tap "Return Card" if the transaction needs to be cancelled. (Courtesy of Joanna Espiritu and Ciera Earl.)

Figure 11.64

This screen shows that the user has inserted the wrong PIN. (Courtesy of Joanna Espiritu and Ciera Earl.)

11. Mobile, Desktop, and Custom Apps

Figure 11.65

This screen shows that the user has inserted the correct PIN. (Courtesy of Joanna Espiritu and Ciera Earl.)

Figure 11.66

The structure of the main screen after entering the correct PIN provides a clear organization of the main options and allows the user to see their savings and checking. (Courtesy of Joanna Espiritu and Ciera Earl.)

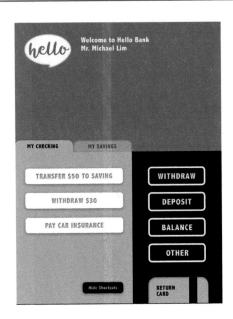

Figure 11.67

Layout inside the Checking section. (Courtesy of Joanna Espiritu and Ciera Earl.)

Figure 11.68

Choosing the "Withdraw" option. (Courtesy of Joanna Espiritu and Ciera Earl.)

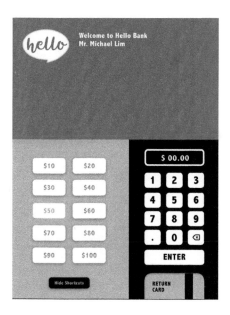

Figure 11.69

A keypad is provided to enter the amount the user wishes to receive. (Courtesy of Joanna Espiritu and Ciera Earl.)

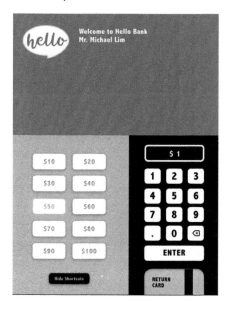

Figure 11.70

Creating five pages will set the price to $15. (Courtesy of Joanna Espiritu and Ciera Earl.)

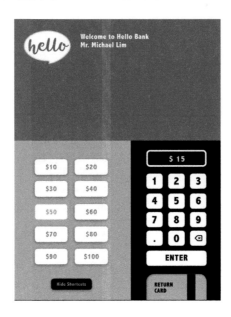

Figure 11.71

InDesign page that shows "$15." (Courtesy of Joanna Espiritu and Ciera Earl.)

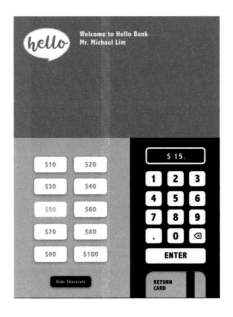

Figure 11.72

InDesign page that shows "$15." (Courtesy of Joanna Espiritu and Ciera Earl.)

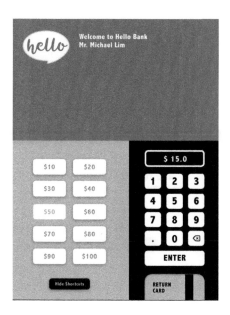

Figure 11.73

InDesign page that shows "$15.0." (Courtesy of Joanna Espiritu and Ciera Earl.)

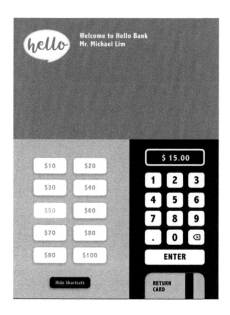

Figure 11.74

InDesign page that shows "$15.00." (Courtesy of Joanna Espiritu and Ciera Earl.)

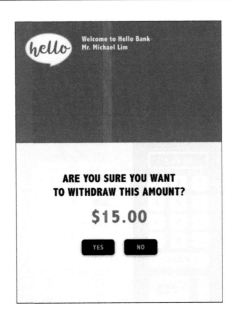

Figure 11.75

Security question prior to the withdrawal. (Courtesy of Joanna Espiritu and Ciera Earl.)

Figure 11.76

Order being processed design. (Courtesy of Joanna Espiritu and Ciera Earl.)

11. Mobile, Desktop, and Custom Apps

Figure 11.77

Taking cash from the ATM interface. (Courtesy of Joanna Espiritu and Ciera Earl.)

Figure 11.78

Options after withdrawing money from the ATM. (Courtesy of Joanna Espiritu and Ciera Earl.)

Figure 11.79

Interface animation after clicking the "Print Only" option. (Courtesy of Joanna Espiritu and Ciera Earl.)

Figure 11.80

Proving other options. (Courtesy of Joanna Espiritu and Ciera Earl.)

11. Mobile, Desktop, and Custom Apps

Figure 11.81

Reminder to take the card from the ATM. (Courtesy of Joanna Espiritu and Ciera Earl.)

Figure. 11.82

ATM app provides with an ending message. (Courtesy of Joanna Espiritu and Ciera Earl.)

SECTION IV
Exporting Testing-Ready Prototypes (and Other Export Options)

12

Exporting Files

You can export files from InDesign in various formats, including PDF, ePub, and Adobe Viewer.

Saving as a PDF (Interactive)

To save an interactive PDF version of your file, first go to "File" in the main menu > select "Export" > and in the drop menu at the bottom (Figure 12.1), select "Adobe PDF (Interactive)."

Figure 12.1

Exporting Adobe PDF (Interactive). After selecting Adobe PDF (Interactive), click "Save."

The "Export to Interactive PDF" window (Figure 12.2) has many options. Starting with "General," there are options to export "All" pages, a certain "Range" of pages, "Pages," or "Spreads." This chooses how the PDF will be displayed on the screen.

Under "Viewing," meanwhile, there are options for viewing the PDF in different sizes and layouts, such as single page and two-up. Also, a "Presentation" can be automatically opened in full screen if you check the corresponding box.

You should only use page transitions (Figure 12.3) if necessary, because they can hurt the viewer or user, if you choose something that becomes annoying or does not work instead of complementing the design.

Under "Options" (Figure 12.4), you can choose whether or not you want to include all media (by selecting "Include All"), including any audio or video you had embedded in the PDF file. You can choose "Appearance Only" for smaller file,

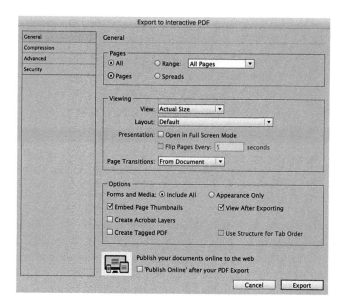

Figure 12.2

After clicking "Save," a window will appear titled "Export to Interactive PDF."

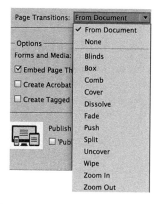

Figure 12.3

Page transitions are found under "Viewing."

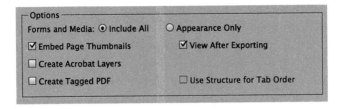

Figure 12.4

Underneath Page Transitions, in a section called "Options," you can choose "Include All," "Appearance Only," and other options to customize the page transitions. Most likely, you will select the checkboxes, "Embed Page Thumbnails" and "View After Exporting."

with videos or audio not included. "Embed Page Thumbnails" allows you to see the thumbnails of the PDF pages. Also, if you check "View After Exporting," it will automatically open the file in *Acrobat*. "Create Adobe Layers" exports your layers, and allows you to turn on and off layers in the Acrobat PDF. The "Create Tagged PDF" option allows you to export the content of the presentation, keeping its design style when you copy and paste, including whether text is bold or italic, and so on.

The last checkbox at the bottom (Figure 12.2) is "'Publish Online' after PDF export," Using this option, you can return to InDesign, where the following window (Figure 12.5) will appear to give you the option to share the document with others on desktop, tablet, or mobile devices through an online URL link.

Figure 12.5

After selecting "Publish Online" from the top menu, a window will automatically appear, titled "Publish Your Document Online."

Publish Online

The window to publish documents online has two options, General and Advanced. General offers simple, step-by-step options for whether you want to export and view as single or spread pages, "Allow viewers to download the document as a PDF (print)," and, if you want privacy, you can check the box "Hide and Embed options in the published document." After everything is set, click or tap "Publish."

If you want to explore the advanced section, select the "Advanced" tab. There, you can change the cover for all social postings (Facebook, Twitter, and Email) or choose other pages inside the presentation. In addition, using the "Choose Image" option allows you to choose any image outside the presentation (as a separate file) as a cover instead of the first page of the InDesign document (Figure 12.6).

In the "Image Settings," you can choose from JPEG, GIF, and PNG formats. "Resolution" provides three options: Low (72 PPI), Standard (96 PPI), and HiDPI (144 PPI). When choosing a resolution, make sure all the images in InDesign have the same resolution so the exported file stays consistent. You cannot convert a 72PPI to a 144 PPI, because it will instantly show the original, low resolution. If you are using 144 PPI, then, make sure your image files are saved to at least 144 PPI resolution. "JPEG Image quality" provides four options: Low, Medium, High, and Maximum. The "GIF Options Palette" provides Adaptive (no dither), System (Mac), Web, and System (Win). These options help with any low-resolution GIF images. Last, for the PDF (Print) format, you can even choose the type of PDF

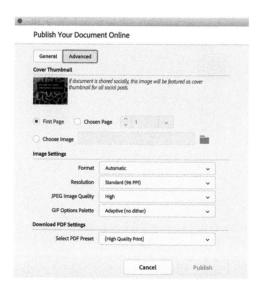

Figure 12.6

The "Advanced" settings in Publish Your Document Online provide more options, such as the cover thumbnail, image settings, and PDF download settings.

file that the viewer or user will download (Figure 12.7). Viewers and users with access to the InDesign URL link can download a PDF (Print) only if you check the box, "Allow viewers to download the document as a PDF (Print)," located toward the bottom of the window in the "General" Tab (Figures 12.8 through 12.10).

Figure 12.7

With the image quality drop-down menu open, there are many options, depending on the publishing target, whether print or digital.

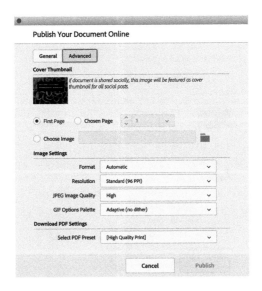

Figure 12.8

Advanced section in the window, Publish Your Document Online. On the options shown selected, there is no extra cover; viewing proceeds directly to the first page. Also, the image format is automatic, image quality is high, and the PDF download will be in high quality for print.

Figure 12.9

After clicking "Publish," the file is uploaded to the web on the indd.adobe.com website as shown earlier. Make sure to copy the link for future viewing of the PDF file online.

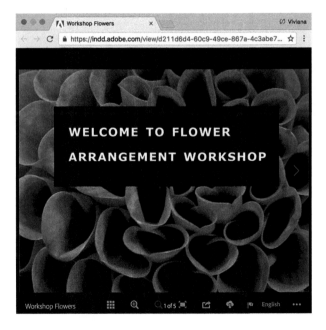

Figure 12.10

The online file is now available now and can be shared through the URL, seen from anywhere and also downloaded, if allowed.

In online view of the PDF (Interactive) version, you can see the presentation. Online view provides a menu at the bottom, from left to right: the title of the file; icon that, when clicked, shows thumbnails of the pages at the bottom at once; zoom in; zoom out; full screen; share; download PDF; report abuse; language options of Deutsch, English, French, and Chinese; turn sound on and off and volume; and embed.

Saving File as an EPUB (Fixed Layout)

An EPUB file can be published in places such as iBooks. This standard file format is broadly known for its use as e-magazines and e-books, but it can also preview prototypes for websites and apps (Figures 12.11 through 12.22).

Figure 12.11

From the top menu, select "File" > then "Export..."

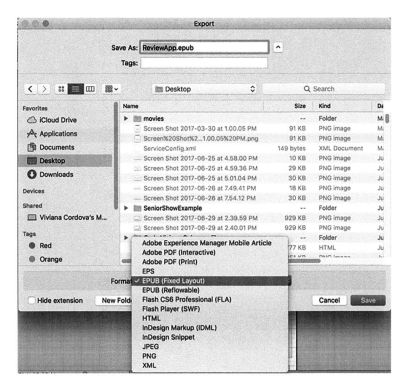

Figure 12.12

In the "Export" window, select "EPUB (Fixed Layout)" from the Format menu and click "Save."

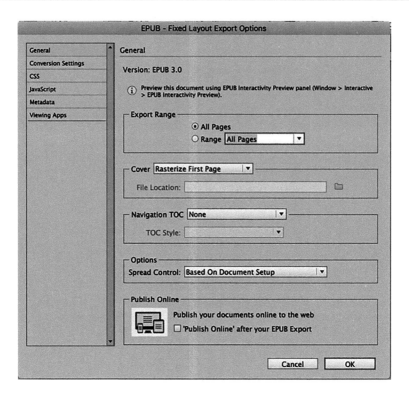

Figure 12.13

The EPUB—Fixed Layout Export Options window will ask you whether you want to export all pages or only some, and whether you have a cover and a Table of Contents (TOC). Once you are done making these choices, click "OK."

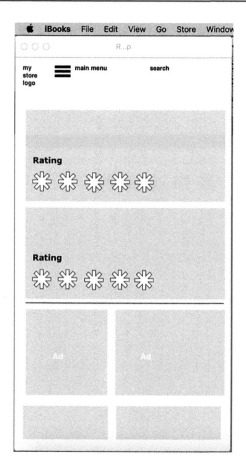

Figure 12.14

If you have a Mac with the iBooks App, the EPUB file will automatically open there.

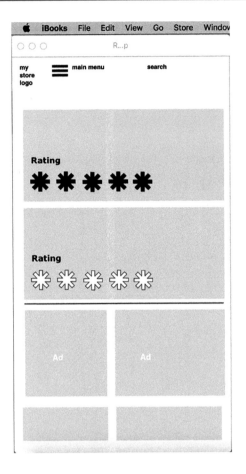

Figure 12.15

If you are exporting a website or app, the animations and interactions will function similarly to the Publish Online option.

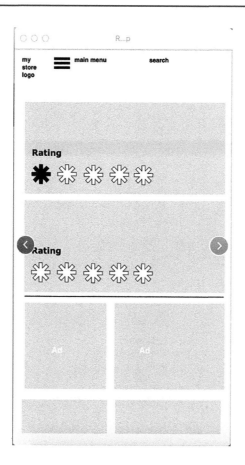

Figure 12.16

You can also navigate with arrows from left to right, which is something that iBook provides.

Saving File as a Flash Player (SWF)

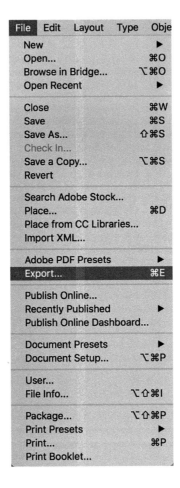

Figure 12.17

From the top menu, select "File" > then "Export."

Figure 12.18

Once the Export window opens, select "Flash Player (SWF)."

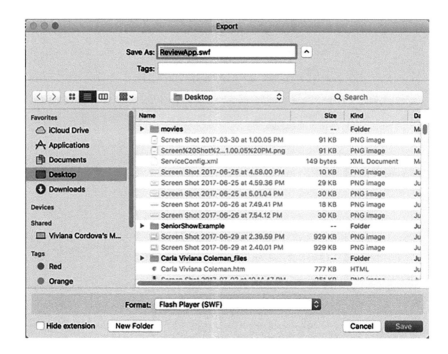

Figure 12.19

After selecting the Flash Player (SWF) format, click "Save."

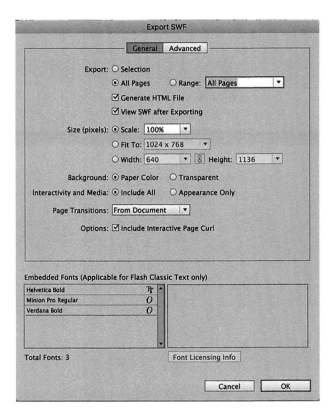

Figure 12.20

The "Export SWF" window opens, providing a wide range of options from which to choose. First, decide if you want to export all pages, if you want an HTML file, and if you want to see the SWF after exporting. It also gives you the option to change the scale of the document to a percentage smaller than 100% width and height. It also asks whether or not you want to keep the background or include all media. Finally, it asks if you want the page transitions from the document. Once you have made all of those choices, click "OK."

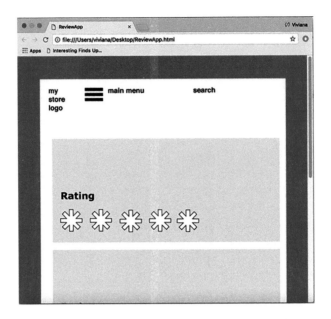

Figure 12.21

The SWF file opens in an HTML page from the local host (desktop).

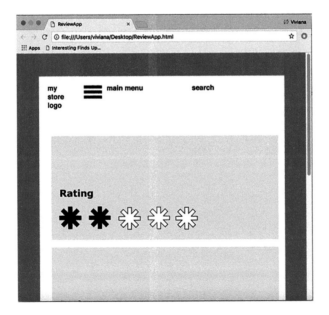

Figure 12.22

Interaction given to the file should work properly.

12. Exporting Files

Saving a File as InDesign Markup (IDML)

Saving an IDML file is extremely helpful when sharing a file with someone who has an older or later version of InDesign. IDML files can be opened by InDesign CS4 and later, but not lower versions. Also, you are highly encouraged to save a Package version, which will keep all the files organized. To save a Package file, go to the top menu "File" > then select "Package." InDesign will automatically retrieve everything (Figures 12.23 through 12.25).

Figure 12.23

From the top menu, select "File" > then "Save As."

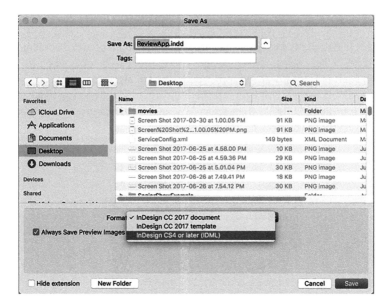

Figure 12.24

From the "Save As" window, select from the Format drop-down menu, "InDesign CS4 or later (IDML)." Then, click "Save."

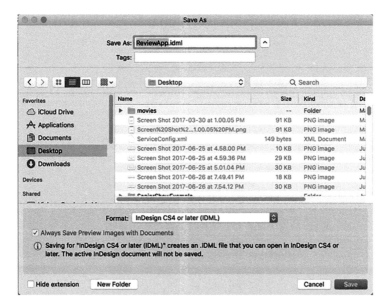

Figure 12.25

Save the IDML file in the folder where all the images, fonts, and other files are saved.

Saving File as a JPEG

JPEG files are great to send to a developer or someone else who might need every-thing in one layer and a small file size (Figures 12.26 through 12.30).

Figure 12.26

From the top menu, select "File" > then "Export..."

Figure 12.27

From the Export window, it is recommended to create a new folder. In this example, the new folder is called "JPEGS_Review_App." Click "Create."

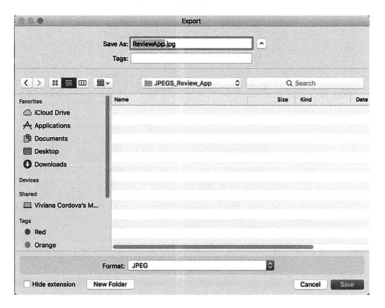

Figure 12.28

The new folder has been created in the Export window for the JPEG files. Now that the location has been created, click "Save" to save the files.

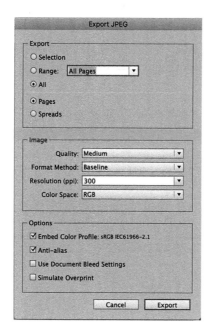

Figure 12.29

From the "Export JPEG" window, you can select all pages or a specific selection. Selecting the right quality of resolution and color space is very important. Once you have made all these choices, click "Export."

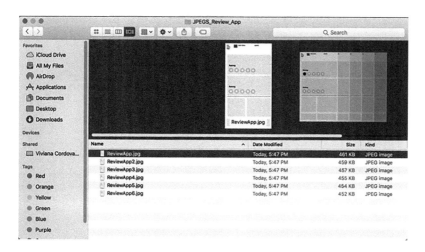

Figure 12.30

Inside the created Folder, all the selected pages are saved as JPEGs.

Saving File as a PNG

Saving as a PNG is necessary only if you are saving pages, icons, or any other content with transparency (Figures 12.31 through 12.35).

Figure 12.31

Go to the top of the main menu, and select "File" > then "Export."

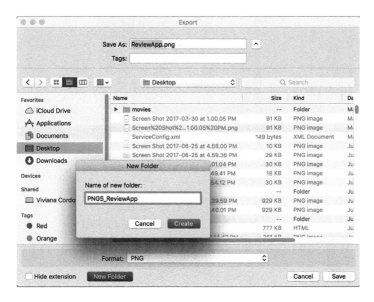

Figure 12.32

In the Export window, click "New Folder" so you can keep all the individual PNG files in order. The above-mentioned folder will be called "PNGs_ReviewApp."

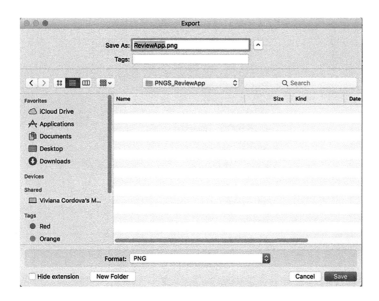

Figure 12.33

Now that the folder has been created in the Export window, select "PNG" from the Format drop-down menu and click "Save."

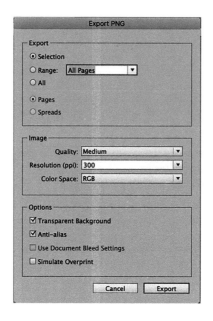

Figure 12.34

The Export PNG window will appear, providing options to export either all pages or selected ones. You can change image quality, resolution, and color; most importantly, make sure to check the box for Transparent Background. After making all your choices, click "Export."

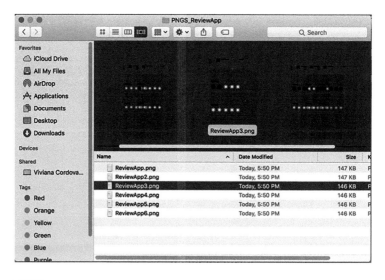

Figure 12.35

The PNG folder holds all of the saved images, and all of them have transparent backgrounds.

12. Exporting Files

Index

Note: Page numbers followed by f refer to figures.

M